Praise for *The Workshop Book*

'An outstanding how-to manual that is packed with expert digestible tips – highly recommended.'

Alex Mahon, CEO, The Foundry

'An excellent resource for managers, lecturers and students alike. It is well researched and packed full of practical tips and examples of good and bad practice, and will turn those wasted meetings into productive and creative workshops. This will become the 'go to' book for anyone planning a workshop.'

Dr Deborah Shaw, Reader in Film Studies at the University of Portsmouth

'Pamela Hamilton has years of hard-earned experience on what makes workshops work – and fail. An essential primer for anyone trying to brainstorm ideas and concepts, and for getting the best out of teams.'

Ben Page, Chief Executive, Ipsos MORI

'This book should be in every facilitator's toolkit. It fits perfectly with Pret's learning culture; simple and effective.'

Ian Watson, Group Head of Pret Academy, Pret a Manger

'This is a fantastic, insightful, one-stop shop for running workshops. It combines the theory and practical insights perfectly. A book I will constantly be using.'

Fran Merrylees, HR Director Online, Pay and Interactive at ITV

'The Workshop Book is wonderfully practical and full of sensible suggestions, tips and hints of how to run successful workshops. It is a book that you will use again and again. The author's personal stories also add an empathetic touch.'

Jennifer Whyte, Global CMI Director, Unilever

'If you're responsible for the creative health of your organisation, then you'd better get your hands on this book. Better yet, commit it to heart. And practice, practice, practice all the techniques. It'll lead to more productive workshops, it'll yield more dynamic and engaging ideas, and it'll promote the importance of creativity with your company!'

Pele Cortizo-Burgess, Global Chief Creative Officer, MEC and President, L'Equipe L'Oréal

PEARSON

At Pearson, we believe in learning – all kinds of learning for all kinds of people. Whether it's at home, in the classroom or in the workplace, learning is the key to improving our life chances.

That's why we're working with leading authors to bring you the latest thinking and best practices, so you can get better at the things that are important to you. You can learn on the page or on the move, and with content that's always crafted to help you understand quickly and apply what you've learned.

If you want to upgrade your personal skills or accelerate your career, become a more effective leader or more powerful communicator, discover new opportunities or simply find more inspiration, we can help you make progress in your work and life.

Every day our work helps learning flourish, and wherever learning flourishes, so do people.

To learn more, please visit us at **www.pearson.com/uk**

The Workshop Book

How to design and lead successful workshops

PAMELA HAMILTON

Harlow, England • London • New York • Boston • San Francisco • Toronto • Sydney • Auckland • Singapore • Hong Kong
Tokyo • Seoul • Taipei • New Delhi • Cape Town • São Paulo • Mexico City • Madrid • Amsterdam • Munich • Paris • Milan

PEARSON EDUCATION LIMITED
Edinburgh Gate
Harlow CM20 2JE
United Kingdom
Tel: +44 (0)1279 623623
Web: www.pearson.com/uk

First published 2016 (print and electronic)

Pearson Education is not responsible for the content of third-party internet sites.

ISBN: 978-1-292-11970-0 (print)
        978-1-292-11972-4 (PDF)
        978-1-292-11973-1 (ePub)

British Library Cataloguing-in-Publication Data
A catalogue record for the print edition is available from the British Library

Library of Congress Cataloging-in-Publication Data
A catalog record for the print edition is available from the Library of Congress

10 9 8 7 6 5 4 3 2
20 19 18 17

Cover design by Two Associates

Print edition typeset in 9.5pt ITC Giovanni by Lumina Datamatics
Print edition printed in Great Britain by Ashford Colour Press Ltd

NOTE THAT ANY PAGE CROSS REFERENCES REFER TO THE PRINT EDITION

Contents

About the author

I first learned about workshops in early 2000 when I was a junior insights manager at Unilever. I went on a creative problem-solving course that gave me my first workshop experience, and it inspired me to learn more. At the time, collaborative and creative ways of working were the preserve of the design and advertising gurus, not serious (boring) market researchers like us. But thanks to the Osborn-Parnes Creative Problem Solving Process, Edward de Bono, and companies like Synectics and ?What If!, workshops have become a common approach across all types of organisations.

I have been designing and leading workshops in the 15 years since. I have run thousands of workshops all over the world, about laundry, diamonds, deodorants, ice cream, stock cubes, TV soap operas, handbags, home insurance, computer systems, digital behaviour, coffee, supermarkets, fizzy drinks, news reporting and lots of food projects. I've worked with teenagers, older people, VIPs, scientists, artists and experts, and I've led workshops for 3 people to 600 people.

I was MD of Research International's Innovation Bureau and Head of Creative Development at ITV Imagine, and I founded the Workshop Cookbook creative development consultancy. We run workshops and train people to lead workshops for big and small companies around the world.

I'm still curious about how and why workshops work, and continue to read psychology, neuroscience and collective intelligence research to keep us working better together. I believe the need for workshops is more important now than ever before. This book is a distillation of the workshop approach I've developed based on my experience so far.

Acknowledgements

I have been very lucky to work with, and learn from, many clever people. This book is the sum of the relationships and experiences I've had with these talented professionals, and I hope it does them justice.

I was working by myself as a filing clerk in a room filled from floor to ceiling with archive boxes, when Monica Juanas rescued me and introduced me to the world of market research. Ashwin Malhotra told me what a workshop was and sent me on that first training course in creative problem solving. Clare Thompson, Bruce Robertson and Pele Cortizo-Burgess gave me the courage to set out on my own in the right direction.

There are people I've worked with along the way who continue to inspire and challenge me (in a good way!), including Alexandra Wren, Jen Whyte, Amber D'Albert, Annette Mathers, Helen Wing, Sue Phillips, Ricardo Arantes, Nicola Davis, Mita Shaha, Billie Ing, Ollie Sweet, Wendy Adams, Sam Matthewson and Colin Woodcock.

I must thank my Workshop Cookbook team, who have learned every lesson and experienced every mistake alongside me, with laughter and sometimes tears, and at all hours of the day and night. Thank you Richard Evans, who draws everything we do, Alison Darling, who runs the business so well, Anna Johnson, who helped me write the book, and Min Wright and Ian Roe, who make sure we can pay for everything. The Portsmouth Cultural Trust kindly host my writing nest, and I am very thankful for their support.

Thank you to those brave people who read the first couple of drafts and gave us invaluable feedback, including Sue Soan, Sue Phillips, Vanessa Otake, Jen Whyte, Paul Bennett, Katherine Richards, Min Wright, Alison Darling, Sara Kortenray, John Gamp, Colin Hosie and Robin Tucker. Thank you also to Penny Bennett for styling and Katie Hyams for photography, as well as to Strathclyde University and Anne Pringle for fact checking.

Thank you to my daughter Bailey for her excellent and funny ideas, and to Kasia and Charlie Bennett, Ian Wright and Tamlyn Norcott for encouraging me along the way. And finally to my husband Paul, who quite literally made the book possible with his advice, encouragement and the confidence he has in me.

Find more about us and the Workshop Academy at:
www.workshopcookbook.com or email info@workshopcookbook.com.

What this book will do for you

The Workshop Book will give you the principles to lead a productive and creative workshop that enhances the collective intelligence of your team. Time to think together is vital. To solve a problem, a team should be able to create better ideas than the most intelligent person in the group could do alone.[1] This book will give you everything you need to make this happen, in every workshop, big or small.

What this book will give you:

▶ The tools you need to design and lead successful workshops yourself.

▶ Basic workshop plans for every objective, that you can use immediately.

▶ Ways to keep your team focused and engaged.

▶ Advice for dealing with difficult workshops or participants.

The chapters are grouped into three sections – design, lead and action:

1 **Design:** the preparation, design and reasoning behind structuring workshops in a specific way.

2 **Lead:** how to create a productive mood in your workshop to keep it focused and under control.

3 **Action:** the workshop tools you can use for different objectives, with an example workshop plan for each (downloadable at www.workshopcook book.com).

This is a reference manual for you to use again and again for tools and inspiration, so do skip to the relevant section. Throughout the book you will find a number of tools and workshop plans for you to adapt to your objective. At the end of each chapter there are some questions to ask yourself as a workshop leader.

1

An introduction to workshops

What is a workshop?

A workshop is a collaborative working session in which a team achieves an agreed goal together. The goal could be to solve a problem, create ideas, work through an issue or find agreement between team members.

Workshops differ from conventional meetings in that they use a structured creative approach and so have a different type of agenda and behaviours. However, workshop principles can be used to improve even everyday meetings.

Running a workshop is like being both the chef and the host of an important meal. Like any good chef, you wouldn't turn up to a kitchen and hope to find the right ingredients. Good meals, like workshops, involve careful planning and preparation, skill in the cooking of the meal on the day, as well as timely delivery of all of the courses to keep your demanding guests satisfied.

Workshops compete with people's time, so a workshop leader needs to plan and lead so that the goal is achieved within the time allowed.

Who can run a workshop?

Anyone can run a workshop, but with planning and structure you can lead a brilliant workshop. Meetings that need to create a specific output or decision require a leader who will take on an evolved chairperson role and supercharge the time for productivity and creativity, by turning the meeting into a workshop.

The workshop leader need not be the same person each time, nor the most important person in the room. They simply need to take responsibility for inviting the right people, planning how the time will be used, preparing stimuli to inspire ideas or output and leading the session in a way that keeps the whole team contributing throughout.

It is often the most passionate, organised or entrepreneurial people who volunteer to lead workshops, although less experienced and introverted people can do an equally great job with the right tools and planning.

Why workshops are useful in a digital world

Technology has given us efficiency, connectivity, access to information and greater potential for creativity. In many cases this has given us knowledge, research and collaboration that was previously impossible. However, our devices are making us more insular. We are often remote, spending less time face to face even when sitting in the same office. We are often time and attention starved.

We are much more likely to have clever ideas if we properly collaborate and curate them. Unfortunately, the way we now work in a digital world is a daily challenge to idea creation. Time to think is vital, but switching between tasks and technologies can distract us from progressive thought, and has been proved to limit our ideas and intelligence.[1] We need to be careful not to let technology disrupt the time and attention we invest in developing ideas.

Meetings in person have become more valuable to us, even if (and maybe because) we are busier and have less time to schedule them. We need to acknowledge the importance of our face-to-face time and make sure that we get the most out of our team members' interaction with each other.

Workshops provide structure

Modern business is more collaborative and less hierarchical than in the past. Traditionally a chairperson would prepare an agenda, refer to previous minutes and make sure the order of business was covered and actions agreed. Not all meetings need a chairperson, but when a meeting has to achieve a specific goal, it does need structure.

'A committee is a cul-de-sac down which ideas are lured and then quietly strangled.'

Sir Barnett Cocks

Unstructured meetings rely on group consensus rather than the leadership of one authority figure, and consensus-driven ideas are not always the best ones.[2] At worst, compromise can create blandness. A well-led workshop is the best way to help a team achieve a goal together.

Is it a workshop or not?

The word 'workshop' is used across industries to describe many different types of working session. However, the term is over-used. There are success factors that make a workshop, and danger signs that your session is not one.

Success factors that make a workshop	Danger signs that it is not a workshop
There is a clear objective to achieve.	There is no clear goal or output.
There is a reason why it needs to be a workshop.	The goal could be achieved in a regular meeting.
There is a clearly structured agenda.	It is a brainstorm.
It is designed and run by a workshop leader.	It is a collaborative session without a leader.
Everyone attending has brought some ideas or inspiration to the session.	People start thinking about the objective when they walk into the room.
The session brings new angles and fresh stimulus to the objective.	There is no new information or inspiration in the session.
People enjoy being there.	It feels chaotic or stressful to be there.
It enhances the team's collective intelligence.	It is dominated by one or two team members.
It stands alone as an event, and devotes the right amount of time to achieving the objective.	It is a small section at the end of a big conventional meeting.

Ask yourself

▶ Does technology distract your team?

▶ Do you feel some meetings would be better run as workshops?

▶ Do you think your team could be helped to be more creative or productive?

Design

Designing your workshop

The design of a workshop is as important as the delivery. This section will provide you with the reasoning behind structuring workshops in a specific way. Once the principles of workshop design are clear, you can create your own tools and techniques to suit your team and objectives.

2 CHAPTER TWO
The workshop approach

Workshops use a method of creative thinking. The creative thinking method is a way of approaching a topic in a new way, in order to find new solutions. We often hope that we will come up with great ideas immediately, but if we focus too early on finding the right answer, we cut short our creative thinking. We stop ourselves from creating truly great ideas if we limit how ambitious we are at the beginning.

'The best way to have a good idea is to have lots of ideas.'

Linus Pauling

The key to creating great ideas is to have lots of ideas first – even if most of the ideas are not right, they lead to others that are. Even if you are coming up with ideas that are too ambitious or impossible to implement, those ideas can lead to fresh thinking and solutions that are feasible. It is not possible to do creative thinking at the same time as evaluative thinking, and so a workshop leader needs to consider how to keep these thinking styles separate.

Creative thinking

There are four main ways of thinking that are applied in the creative process:

1 **Divergent thinking** is all about creative elaboration, going wide in thinking and exploring many options.
2 **Convergent thinking** is about narrowing down, choosing the right answers and prioritising ideas.[1]
3 **Analysis** is applying your knowledge and expertise to the idea themes and working out which are the most important elements that need to be expressed clearly.

4 **Synthesis** is the expression or wording of those ideas in a manner that makes them clear and easily understood by other people so that they can be acted upon in some way.

For every workshop, whether for 10 people or 100 people, there is a simple method that applies these four styles of thinking – see the table below. This method can be applied over two hours or even two days, on any topic.

	Purpose	Approach	Thinking style	Output
Stage 1: **CREATE** (60% of the workshop time)	To create many options and possibilities of early ideas.	Apply creative thinking in several rounds of idea generation.	Divergent thinking, creative and spontaneous, creating many possibilities, with no evaluation or critical thinking.	An extensive list of ideas and directions.
Stage 2: **EVALUATE** (10% of the workshop time)	To look at all the options and consider the best individual ideas and any themes within the ideas.	Discuss as a team, identify key themes or vote on favourite ideas.	Convergent thinking, evaluating the ideas against objectives and feasibility, and choosing the best themes or options for further development.	A list of important idea themes and some of the best individual ideas.
Stage 3: **DEVELOP** (30% of the workshop time)	To take the best ideas and themes and develop them into fully thought-through ideas.	Choose the top ideas and split into teams to develop these further.	Analysis and synthesis, working through the top ideas and themes to combine the best elements and express the essence of the idea.	A short list of the best ideas, well expressed and clear, with ideas for actions and next steps.

In the early stages of creative thinking there is no 'right' answer. It is in the journey of searching for and creating many answers that creativity blossoms. Every workshop, whether it be strategic or creative, will be more successful if it is designed to allow the team to think divergently first, then convergently.[2] This is because divergent thinking helps create lots of possibilities that are generated without limitations. Once there are many ideas on the table, convergent thinking can be applied to link and theme them into some key ideas.

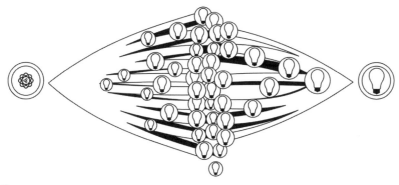

Divergent, convergent

Workshop ingredients

There are key ingredients that make a workshop successful. We will cover these in much more detail in the following chapters.

For successful design:

▶ **Structure:** plan exercises in small teams to allow the topic to be approached from different angles by different groups of people.

▶ **Diversity:** invite a range of participants to make sure you have a team with diverse genders, backgrounds, opinions and ethnicities.

▶ **Stimulus:** create inspiration from new or unusual sources to bring topics to life or stimulate thinking beyond the obvious.

For successful participation:

▶ **Prep task:** use time wisely by having the team do some thinking in advance and bring ideas with them to kick-start the session.

▶ **Focus:** consider how to keep people focused and thinking deeply by being careful not to overwhelm them with information and keeping outside distractions (such as emails or phone calls) to a minimum.

▶ **Behaviour:** encourage positive, constructive behaviours such as conversational turn taking within the workshop.

▶ **Conflict:** plan for constructive conflict, polarised views and challenges as a healthy process to create ideas.

The following chapters in Design, Lead and Action will give you much more detail on how to use these for your workshops.

Ask yourself

▶ Are we creating enough ideas before we choose the best ones?

▶ Are we looking at the issue from several different angles when we create new ideas?

▶ Have we separated the creating from the evaluating in the session?

3

Setting the workshop objective

Unlike everyday meetings, workshops are set up for a specific goal, to solve a problem or to create a defined output. This means that you need to be very clear about what you want the workshop to achieve. Investigating the issue and working out the goal of the workshop improves the workshop design.

The way you ask the question has a big influence on the way the question will be answered.[1] Defining the objective properly means you will set up the workshop for greater success.

Plan with the main stakeholder

Identifying your key stakeholder or 'problem owner' is important. This could be your boss, the person who asked you to lead the session, your client or your fellow team members. The stakeholders are people who will brief you, work with you on the approach and challenge you to get the best from the team. This means spending time working through the issues and objectives with them.

Be wary if there's no stakeholder committing to the workshop or taking the actions afterwards – chances are the workshop won't achieve its objective. If they are a 'problem moaner' (would prefer to spend time on what the problems and barriers are) instead of a 'problem owner' (wants to invest time in solving the issues and moving to action), then the goal may not be met.

In my experience, if stakeholders don't want to commit time or attention to working through the approach, they will show the same lack of commitment during and after the workshop, which means the workshop will not be successful.

'By failing to prepare, you are preparing to fail.'

Benjamin Franklin

Lesson learned: finding the real stakeholder

The least successful workshop I ever led was for a global household cleaning company in its Asian markets. I'd spent some time working with my client on the objectives, the session outline, the stimulus we would use and the approach we would take. I flew out to Malaysia and walked into day 1 of the workshop only to realise, too late, that the client I had prepared with was not the real stakeholder. Her boss was, and he did not want to be in a workshop.

I did my usual enthusiastic set-up of the session, talking through creative behaviours and approaches. He stayed on his laptop without participating at all, except when he heard an idea he didn't like, when he would dismiss it loudly and go back to his emails. His team said less and less, and I tried my best to keep going, hoping everything was going to work out. Unsurprisingly, the workshop did not work. I realised too late that my client was trying to use me to influence her boss, but without being prepared for that I could not.

What should I have done instead? I always ask who else will be in the workshop and make sure I understand their role and influence. I make sure to talk with the bosses before they attend, and check they will participate constructively. After the first hour of the failing session, I should have said to my client that the workshop was not going to succeed and either given the team their time back to use how they wanted to, or asked the boss to leave us to it and come back when we'd created something.

Finding the real objective

Workshop leaders have a privileged position of influence. Even if your stakeholder is your main client, you have a responsibility to everyone in the workshop to help them genuinely achieve something as a collective. Workshops are collaborative processes, and they are powerful because people leave feeling they have created something together. Your stakeholder should be prepared to accept the team's ideas rather than simply trying to push their own.

It is sometimes hard to establish the real objective behind the stated one. For example, your stakeholder may say they want an alignment session, when they really want to make the team agree with their view on how to move things forward. Or you are brought in to run a strategy workshop but what they really need is a team-building session. If you can see that there are hidden or unstated objectives in play, explore those with the team members in advance.

'How to…' tool

A very simple exercise I often use is the 'how to…'

1 Rephrase the workshop objective as a sentence starting with 'How to…' Come up with as many statements as possible – at least 10, if not 20, so that you think divergently about the goal and go beyond the obvious.

2 Write each of your statements on a separate Post-it note.

3 Group your Post-its into similar groups.

4 Choose the group you feel best represents the opportunity that the workshop creates and rewrite the objective based on that group.

You can also run this as a workshop exercise with the whole team, within a workshop, if you want them to create an objective or question that is inspiring and directional.

A 'How to…' example

Initial objective: 'The goal of the workshop is to understand the customer survey feedback and create some ways for us to improve our service in future.'

Rephrase this in at least 10 'how to…' statements, for example:

1 How to make sure the team understand the feedback.

2 How to make sure the team don't get stuck in the negative and can move onto ideas for improvement.

3 How to keep the team encouraged and constructive despite the negative feedback.

4 How to use the negative feedback as an opportunity for new ways of working.

5 How to make sure the team understand the impact of their actions in the past and work out how to make things better in the future.

6 How to make sure we don't get into this situation again.

7 How to make sure we create a completely positive customer experience in future.

8 How to make the team proud of themselves and the service they provide.

9 How to make sure the team feel responsible and accountable for the ideas they create.

10 How to make our team champions of a new, positive customer experience.

Once you've done this you will see that it gives you inspiration for a more exciting, meaningful and inspiring objective, which goes some way to directing the outcomes to be more successful.

As a result of using the 'how to...' tool we could then rephrase the goal as 'the objective of the workshop is to use the customer feedback to inspire ideas that will positively transform the customer experience'.

Can you be both stakeholder and workshop leader?

I believe you can be the leader and the stakeholder, but be very careful in doing so. If you are trying to influence people to do something differently, or if the topic is one they are reluctant to discuss, you are probably not best placed to lead the workshop, because the team won't trust you to do so impartially.

Your main role is to help the team to create and align together, not to impose your view. Will you accept the output if the team create something different from what you believe is the right answer? If so, then go for it. If not, brief someone else to lead the workshop for you; then at least you can participate and give your opinion strongly.

Can you lead and participate in the same workshop?

No. I strongly believe that the workshop leader needs to stay separate from the working group, in order to keep an overview of the session, check participants are on track and sort out any issues. It is very difficult to lead well and participate well at the same time. If there are sections in which you'd like to participate, have another workshop leader who can step in at that point and let you take part.

Ask yourself

▶ What is the objective of the session?

▶ What are the specific physical, deliverable or political outcomes of the session?

▶ How do you want the participants to feel during and after the session?

▶ What has worked well or not so well with this team in the past?

▶ What type of tone or personality would you like the day to have?

▶ What would you like people to say about the event afterwards?

4

CHAPTER FOUR

Who to invite to your workshop

The ideal workshop size is between 12 and 20 people. This is a good number to work with, as there are enough people to mix in small groups through the day. With just 12 people, they can be split into groups of 3 or 4 for working sessions. It doesn't matter how big your workshop is, so long as you have the space to split people into groups of 3 or 4 (so if you had 100 people, you'd want separate tables for up to 33 groups).

Group mechanics

Using the right participants in the right way often comes down to group sizes and the combinations of different personalities to achieve the best diversity and contributions. It used to be common in workshops to have a large group of people 'brainstorming', with a facilitator standing at the front of a room by a flipchart easel, writing down ideas that people shouted out. While this can be a good way to get people energised and excited at the beginning of a session, it leaves out those who are introverted, shy, junior or don't speak the language as confidently as others. And as soon as people feel left out, they lose interest and get bored.

Instead I prefer to have people work in smaller groups of three, creating a combined set of ideas to present back to the main group. I reorder the groups for each new round of ideas, with everyone working with someone new and with new inspiration or tools per round.

Over a workshop day, start with groups of four or five (which allows those less confident to become familiar with the process), then reduce group sizes for each round through the day, down to four, three, and then pairs and even

17

individuals for some exercises. It's easier to do pairs and individual exercises at the end of the day because people are then familiar with the behaviours and know what to do.

Who you invite is more important than how many

The single most important difference to workshop success is the kind of people you invite, not just how many. The people participating in your workshop will make all the difference to its success. Research has found that a greater diversity in gender[1], background and ethnicity[2] leads to higher collective intelligence (when combined with the right creative behaviours).

Even in very international offices, it is sometimes hard to invite a highly diverse group of people to participate, because, by the nature of the company culture, if they work there they will have many things in common. Often we feel we don't have a choice as to who we can invite – if the team already exist, you just invite them, right? Not necessarily. A crucial aspect of workshop design is the make-up of the group itself. I encourage you to take more control over who participates, as it will ensure the time is far better used if you have the right people there.

Easy ways to improve the team

▶ **The same old team:** if you have to invite a certain set of people who work on the topic a lot, consider who else you can invite from within the company to balance them out. Even if those people are very junior, inexperienced or unfamiliar with the project, they will bring fresh thinking.

▶ **A homogeneous team:** if all your participants share the same background, culture or gender, consider how you can get them in the shoes of someone else, by a prep task or personal experience that helps them see other perspectives.

▶ **An ivory tower team:** when the team are far removed from their customers, they are unlikely to create very relevant ideas for them. Think about recruiting extra people to be in the room to represent your customers, business partners, end users or just regular people.

Research on diversity in working groups

▶ **Diversity of culture:** an experiment with financial traders in Singapore and Texas found that culturally and ethnically diverse groups performed significantly better in financial trading than those who were in homogeneous groups.[3] This is likely to be because diverse groups are more challenging and questioning of each other's ideas and so create a higher quality of output.

▶ **Diversity of experience:** research has shown that people with international experience (who have lived in several different cultures or identify with more than one culture) are better problem solvers and are more creative.[4]

▶ **Polarised views:** studies on decision making have shown that groups in which two leaders have polarised viewpoints eventually make more successful decisions.[5] Processing different views towards one answer makes the end decisions stronger, so long as the group members can work positively and constructively together.

'You can not only understand at a much deeper level the opposing point of view, but learn to articulate your own view much more clearly and effectively.'

Nikki Gamble

As workshop leader, consider improving the group with four elements:

▶ the diversity of the group

▶ their talents and traits

▶ the attitudes they bring

▶ the right approach for the company culture.

The rest of this chapter details each of the above to help you improve your workshop group. Focus on the element that best fits your team and their challenges.

1 Diversity of background

▶ **Different perspectives.** Different cultures, backgrounds or genders mean that instead of just accepting what someone else says because you understand or know them, you might well question them, even for clarity, and it is in that questioning and challenging that ideas are made better.

▶ **Experts.** When you need to access some unique information, or are exploring a truly new area, having someone join as an expert is a great way to include clever thinking that your team might not always have access to.

▶ **Your customers, consumers and end users.** In our busy lives we sometimes forget to think about the real people out there who we are working for. It can be incredibly valuable to invite some of your end users to your session as equal participants. Let them share in the issues and challenges, and co-create the answers with you.

▶ **Internal outsiders.** Bring in people from other teams who don't work on the project but belong to the same company. Ensure they are well briefed and prepared to participate – they don't need to be experts, they just need to have opinions and ideas and be comfortable taking part.

2 Talents and traits

▶ **Ability to converse and digest.** It is the ability to take it in turns to share views, as well as the ability to digest other people's ideas and build on them, that increases collective intelligence.[6] Choose the individuals who are most talented at these behaviours.

▶ **Openness to new ideas.** Some people are naturally more open to new concepts and ideas. If you have a choice, opt for those who are interested in new information, try new products regularly and are curious about the world.

▶ **Opinionated.** The people who attend must have ideas and opinions of their own. We want them to be contributors, catalysts and challengers.

▶ **Creative minded.** It is always wonderful to have some truly creative brains in any session. These are people who are able to think independently, come up with loads of ideas and possibilities, and don't get too bogged down in defining the problem or understanding the detail.

3 Attitude to the project

▶ **Project optimists.** You need people who come in with a wish to create new solutions and ideas, and even if they don't know how this will happen, they are relatively confident it will.

▶ **Constructive pessimists.** These people can be very helpful in the session as they act as the devil's advocate and push for the best solutions. Be careful, though – if people are pessimistic about the project, they can derail any session unless they are genuinely prepared to participate constructively.

▶ **Participating bosses.** It is important to include any major stakeholders or decision makers in the planning of the workshop if they will actively and constructively contribute as equal participants in the workshop.

4 Company or team culture

▶ **Creatives with a capital 'C'.** When working with TV people, ad agencies, start-ups, entrepreneurs, inventors and very innovative company cultures, do as much as you can to put other clever people in front of them, shock and surprise them, and let them create the ideas in their own way.

▶ **Traditionalists.** Old-fashioned, more conservative teams need to be treated with respect. Instead of expecting them to go along with your instructions, give them specific reasons why you are asking them to do things in a certain way. Ask their permission rather than telling them what to do.

▶ **Charities, volunteers, educators and non-profits.** These people and organisations are often internally focused and forget to look outside of their organisation or industry for inspiration. Your role can be to bring in the outside world to inspire them and create some optimism and fresh thinking.

▶ **Teams who strongly disagree with each other.** Be very careful to understand the real issues from all the participants before the session, rather than relying on one version of the truth (usually provided by your key stakeholder).

▶ **Workshop weary.** People who regularly attend workshops get tired of them. Make your sessions the best and they will come to them because they trust that you won't waste their time.

▶ **Chronic lateness.** Because a workshop is highly structured, even a 10-minute delay can be disruptive, and yet in my experience it's relatively common for workshops to start 30 minutes behind schedule.

You need to plan for this and try to prevent lateness if possible – for example, in the invitation say 8.45 a.m. arrival time for a 9 a.m. sharp start.

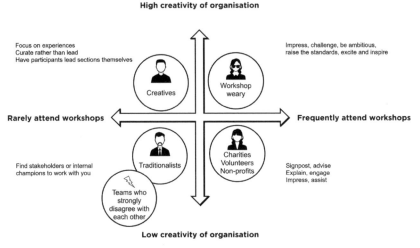

Team culture

People not to invite to your workshop:

▶ **Poppers:** there are two types of poppers: pop-ins and pop-outs. Pop-ins say, 'I have a lot to do that day but I'll pop in at some point'. Pop-outs say, 'I will attend but I'll be popping out for a meeting'. If they pop in late, it means they miss all the set-up, behaviours and objectives; if they pop out, it means you can't rely on them to be fully present.

▶ **Floaters:** these are the people who would prefer to stand back and observe the workshop, participating when they want to. They might be the boss and so don't want to influence working groups, or people who can't fully commit the time. Floaters stop teams from working well together because they have to interrupt their work and update or impress them.

▶ **Disruptors:** it's hard to do but you sometimes have to ask people you know will not be constructive not to attend, and help them to contribute their ideas in advance, or afterwards, instead of disrupting the session.

Showing respect in Japan

I was invited to run a large workshop in Japan, which became one of my favourite projects. The team was a mixture of global (many different cultures) and local (mostly Japanese) team members, who were creating ideas for the Japanese market. We needed to carefully consider how to make sure the main stakeholders, the Japanese, felt comfortable, engaged and able to participate fully, at the same time as allowing the global team to contribute.

I took advice from women in my network who worked between Japan and Western markets. I was warned that being a foreigner, and a woman, I would need to be careful not to offend my clients with direct commands within the workshop, even though as a workshop leader I would need to advise the team how to behave.

▶ **Preparation.** I spoke with each participant in advance of the workshop to get their views on the objective, the ideas they already had and any concerns. Not only was it useful to allow the Japanese team to express their concerns ahead of time, it was also a way of balancing the power between the local experts and the global participants, so that everyone felt heard before we started.

▶ **Translation.** We led the workshop in both English and Japanese (I was the workshop leader, working in English, and my co-facilitator was a Japanese colleague who repeated the set-up and instructions in Japanese). This gave the workshop a feeling of balance and trust.

▶ **Tone.** I was careful to give no direct orders but instead gave each instruction as an invitation to participate. I spoke slowly and respectfully.

Ask yourself

▶ Who has to be there, and who can you invite to balance the group?

▶ Is the group diverse enough?

▶ Are there some fresh perspectives in the room?

▶ What types of people should you design the workshop around?

▶ Is there anyone you need to ask not to attend?

5 Priming the workshop participants

It is important that the people are primed and ready to contribute to a workshop. There are two elements essential to prime people before any workshop:

1 **An invitation:** an invitation that clarifies the objective, sets expectations and builds curiosity and excitement.

2 **A prep task:** an individual task that each participant does in advance of the workshop to kick-start thinking, gather inspiration and prepare each individual to come ready to contribute.

The invitation

People love to get invitations to parties or special occasions, but not to meetings. Because a workshop is different from a meeting, consider how you can make your workshop invitation feel different and more like an invitation they want to receive. For example:

▶ Create a visual invitation with pictures, branding or photos on it, to give a sense of how the workshop will feel or what the topic will be.

▶ Design and print invitations to drop on people's desks instead of emailing them.

▶ Give them something with their invitation, such as a magazine to read to inspire them about the objective, a product to try, an event to attend, a voucher for coffee.

▶ Think about a video invitation, a film of you, or a stakeholder, inviting them to the workshop and explaining how important it is.

▶ Set expectations, such as dress code, or the weather if you're doing anything outside, and warn them you will be limiting phone and laptop use to the breaks.

▶ If you have to book people's time with a calendar invitation, send a separate email explaining the workshop expectations and objective. (If this is sent in the calendar invitation, people often don't read it properly.)

The prep task

Asking participants to do something in advance of the session means they will bring new thinking to the session to inspire new ideas. This prep task is different from a 'pre-read' (when the team leader sends out a huge document for everyone to read before they come).

People often don't do the pre-reading until the last minute, and everyone is reading the same thing, so they all come to the workshop with the same information in mind, which then limits their diverse personal perspectives.

A prep task is better than a pre-read because:

▶ it sets an expectation that this is different from a normal meeting

▶ it makes sure people come ready to contribute to the session

▶ it disrupts hierarchies and factions by putting each participant on the same level

▶ it gets people curious, excited and sometimes competitive

▶ it gets people thinking about the topic earlier

▶ it saves time because information is collected in advance, rather than in the limited time available during the workshop

▶ it brings richer and better informed thinking to the workshop, and provides an immediate source of stimulus to inspire ideas.

What kind of prep task is useful?

The prep task you ask your team to do should be relevant to the workshop objective and encourage each participant to reveal their personal experiences and opinions in a way that will stimulate ideas for the session. You will need to consider how much time people will realistically have, what kinds of tasks they will feel comfortable doing and how to make sure they all do the task.

These are some of the prep tasks I commonly set, all tailored to the workshop objective:

▶ Bring an example of a brand, product or person who talks to our customers in an engaging way, and be prepared to describe why they do this so successfully.

▶ Talk to a friend or family member who is affected by our workshop topic and understand their views, needs and ideas to contribute to the session.

▶ Take some photos of a situation, shops or environment that you believe has solved similar challenges to our workshop topic, and be ready to explain why they have done so.

▶ Think about a moment in your life when you had to make a big choice, how you made that decision and who/what helped you.

▶ Go to an event, experience or place that is an extreme version of our workshop subject and tell us about your experience.

▶ Try a new product for a week in advance of the workshop and come ready to describe your experience.

▶ Read a newspaper or magazine before the workshop and bring your thoughts and observations about the readers of that publication.

▶ Sign up to a new game, website or social media platform that you've never tried before and make notes about your experience.

Prep tasks as ice-breakers

In order to use time well, introduction exercises and ice-breakers should be related directly to the workshop topic. Prep tasks can be very effective as introduction exercises, because they introduce the people to each other and provide new information to the workshop. Consider, therefore, prep tasks that will allow people to share a little about themselves at the beginning of the session as well as creating some inspiration for use later on.

Dos and don'ts of sending out a prep task

Do	Don't
Tell people why it's important.	Let them believe they can do it on the way to the workshop.
Make it inspiring and creative.	Make it onerous or too personally revealing.
Give it a clear structure and template to capture thoughts.	Make it a verbal download.
Make sure everyone does it (even if at the last minute).	Allow prep task abstainers.
Send it a week in advance – this allows for time (and a weekend) for people to prepare their answers.	Send it too early (more than a week in advance) or too late (the day before).

Ask yourself

▶ How can you make people excited about being invited?

▶ Have you set expectations within the invitation?

▶ Is your prep task relevant to the session?

▶ How will you make sure everyone does the prep task?

6
The workshop set-up

Workshops work best if you are able to go to a different venue, away from the office. However, not all projects have catering and venue budgets that allow us to do this. Nevertheless, we can still take control over the set-up and experience to ensure the session is as productive as possible.

Workshop logistics

The workshop leader creates an immersive experience for the participants. It is very important to consider the logistics and allow time to prepare for these (or get some support to help you). I always think about how valuable each person in the workshop is to the organisation, and so how important it is not to waste the organisation's time and money. If the logistics are not right, people will not be able to take part properly.

Logistics can include:

▶ the venue (where you will be hosting the workshop)

▶ printing (templates, posters, documents)

▶ travel (booking taxis, transport or people making their own way)

▶ stationery (Blu-Tack, Sharpies, Post-its, flipcharts)

▶ stimuli (boxes full of interesting items, case studies, reports, collages representing the topic)

▶ recruitment of experts and customers for co-creation (working with customers or experts as equal partners to achieve the workshop objective)

- ▶ technology (laptops, projectors, TVs, AV, microphones for large groups, music, films)
- ▶ decoration and set design (bringing the topic to life in a physical space)
- ▶ event management (for large groups and multi-day workshops).

Visual and spatial memory

Research has found that visual and spatial memories are far stronger than verbal or conversational memories.[1] Actors have been found to be able to remember their lines for a play from years ago far more easily when standing on the same stage in the same theatre in which they acted.[2] Our visual instincts are one of our most powerful because we relied on them for survival. With advances in computer graphics and the ease of sharing pictures and videos, people think more visually than they used to.[3] Using people's visual instinct is a great way to excite, inspire and make a workshop memorable.

The venue

If the workshop is taking place in the same room where you have other meetings, the room itself will keep people in old thinking habits. Consider decorating the room or rearranging it to surprise people and disrupt their habits. Use the workshop to transform the room through the day into a new visual environment. Cover the walls with posters, themes, completed templates, ideas sheets and stimuli, and photograph them to refer to later. This establishes a powerful memory of the journey of the day and what was created.

Do as much as you can to make the space feel different by tidying it up, moving things around, having the team face a different way, opening the windows, decorating the walls and, depending on your audience and company culture, having music playing.

'Multi-sensory environments improve the development of thought, intelligence and social skills.'

Chailey Heritage Foundation

Room set-up

A workshop is an experience you are inviting people to. When you walk into a theatre for a show, you don't want to see the set designers fixing the stage or the actors rehearsing. When the team walk into the workshop, be ready to greet them, make them welcome, let them settle. Don't make them watch you setting up slides, rushing about unpacking materials or writing on flipcharts.

One of the main things I think about when I set up the room is what people will see as soon as they walk in. Is there a prominent wall opposite the door that you can decorate? Are there blinds that have stayed closed for 20 years that you can open to let some light in? And, of course, is the room tidy?

Make sure your meeting rooms are booked at least an hour in advance of the start time to allow you to set up.

Change the room

I once ran a workshop in a small meeting room. There were discarded flipcharts on the floor, old posters on the walls, too many chairs in the room and conference phones, wires, plugs and chargers on the table. Physical clutter has been proven to restrict the brain's processing ability[4] and I believe that mess, clutter and untidiness cause people to become distracted. This means that they are made slightly uncomfortable by it, even if not consciously so.

We weren't allowed to throw anything away, but we did move all of the rubbish outside the room to give us space (promising to put it back again). We took all the technology off the table and laid down neat Post-its, books and pens. We covered the walls with our own beautifully printed posters. We took all the extra chairs out of the room so there was space to sit and move. When the team came into the room, they might not have realised why, but I am certain it made the workshop feel better.

Here's how we set up most workshops:

▶ Cabaret-style seating with 4–6 chairs per table.

▶ Tables positioned informally.

▶ Enough space between tables and chairs to walk comfortably around the room.

▶ No clutter on the tables (flowers, water, drinks, notebooks) unless it specifically relates to the workshop.

▶ Wall space for sticking up flipcharts and decorations.

▶ Flipchart easels for use in breakout sessions.

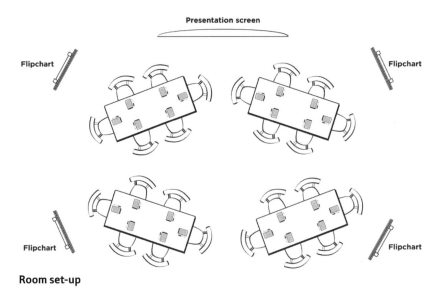

Room set-up

Don't use breakout rooms

Doorway effect

Have you ever gone next door to retrieve something and forgotten what you went there for? Researchers have identified a 'doorway effect' that makes you forget what you were doing when you walk through a doorway.[5] The brain uses what is called an 'event boundary' to let go of some information, such as unnecessary short-term memories, to make space for new thinking, and it does this naturally when we pass through doorways.

I don't like people leaving the room to go into separate breakout sessions. I feel you lose people along the corridors, and they separate themselves from the energy of the main group. It's hard to control more than one room. I prefer to keep everyone in the same space so that they can feed off the energy and noise from the rest of the room, and keep the same pace and mood as each other.

The catering

Workshops are hard work, and people need sustenance. To sustain people's brains and energy we need to give them lots of good, healthy food all day long (and some treats!), such as fruit, juices, salads, lean meats, freshly baked desserts, and good coffee and a choice of teas. These might seem like luxuries, but they are necessary. Sustenance rewards people for working hard. It might also attract them to come in the first place.

Controlling the catering also leaves you in control of people's time. If you aren't able to organise catering, you run the risk of losing people to the canteen or the high street at lunchtime.

Get catering

I ran a workshop for a company in a room in their warehouse. In order to get there we all had to don high-visibility jackets and cross the warehouse floor. We were told that we weren't allowed to order catering (for cost reasons) but that there was a kitchen where we could make some tea. We had a tight schedule and were due to kick off at 9 a.m. When people arrived, there was no water, coffee or even milk for the tea. We lost the team for 20 minutes while they went back to their offices to pick up food, hot drinks and water. I'm sure that the time wasted cost more than the money we would have spent on catering.

The materials

Workshop materials are essential – you can't rely on other people to provide you with the tools of your trade. Like a carpenter arriving without his toolbox, if you arrive at your workshop expecting that someone has provided you with the stationery you need, you may find that there is an important item missing that will stop you from doing a great job.

▶ **Flipchart paper** is necessary, even if you have all your templates printed in advance or are presenting on a screen. Flipcharts give a space for people to think through their ideas, can be used for instructions and are necessary to provide a blank space for theming Post-its. Often meeting rooms have run out of flipchart paper, and it's hard to find more at a moment's notice, especially if you're in someone else's office.

▶ **Sharpies** are vital, not just because they are good quality, don't leak or run out quickly and draw clean, clear lines, but because they make it easier to read handwriting on a Post-it, and they make handwriting so bold, people become more careful of what they write and how.

▶ **Post-its** are very important to the workshop approach because they create individual points of inspiration that can be themed into groups and moved around, disrupting linear thinking. Even though it can feel like a bit of a waste of paper, the benefits of working in a visual spatial way are essential. Make sure you use 3M-branded Post-its. If you don't, you run the risk of all your Post-its falling off and destroying the themes you have created.

▶ **Templates** give people a structured way to conceptualise their thinking and mean they will come up with ideas that are easy to understand and compare with each other. I usually print these in A2 or bigger, to give people enough space in which to write as a group. Printed materials go a long way to making you look structured and professional, which makes participants feel they are in good hands.

▶ **Nametags** are good, even if the team all know each other well. As the leader, it's easier to motivate people if you can use their name, and nametags help them work well together in breakout groups.

▶ **Voting stickers** (like sticker dots, stars, etc.) are a good way to prioritise ideas. Instead of asking people to write a star or dot on ideas they like, give each person an agreed number of stickers which they can use to vote.

I take all my own materials to every workshop, including flipchart paper, Sharpies, Post-its, templates, masking tape, music speakers, camera, extension lead, nametags, voting stickers and a range of stationery.

Why I carry my own materials

One of the most beautiful workshop venues I have ever been in was a palace on the banks of the Bosphorus in Istanbul. The workshop took place in an ornate room in the gardens, as boats sailed by and the sun shone over the city. It was breathtaking, and to make it more exciting I was running a workshop on the topic of diamonds.

My workshop design was based on writing up ideas on lots of flipcharts, sticking them on the wall and asking the team to read through them all and comment. The flipchart paper the venue provided was a continuous plastic loop, not separate sheets of paper. I found I could cut sections out of the plastic loop that were flipchart sized, to write the ideas on, but the plastic was so stiff that the sections popped into small rolls as soon as they were cut. I stuck them to the walls to straighten them out, which worked until the temperature went up in the afternoon, warming the adhesive until all the flipcharts popped off the wall into a pile of plastic rolls again. Which is why I carry my own flipchart paper to workshops.

Ask yourself

- ▶ What venue will be best for the workshop?
- ▶ What visual stimuli can you include?
- ▶ Who will be providing the catering and what food and drink will there be?
- ▶ Have you prepared all the materials you need yourself?
- ▶ Could there be any logistical issues you should prepare for?

Lead

Leading your workshop

Leading a workshop can be enjoyable and rewarding. Anyone can lead a workshop, and so long as they are well prepared, they will display the necessary confidence because they know they've devised the best use of people's time. This section will help you prepare to stay in control and keep participants focused, and give you the best likelihood of workshop success.

7

The workshop leader

There is a certain type of alchemy that happens when you bring together the right people, in the correct setting, with good inspiration and great timing. Although much of the work happens in the design of the event, the workshop leader ignites these ingredients into the best ideas. The best workshops feel enjoyable for participants, and the best workshop leadership seems effortless and authentic.

Being an authentic workshop leader

Anyone can be a great workshop leader. If you have prepared well, you will be confident in your workshop delivery. More than confidence though, people want to trust you as their guide, so consider how to get your delivery just right.

The main lessons I've learned are:

▶ Be yourself – there's no need to invent a new personality.

▶ Be confident and positive, but not over-zealous or wildly optimistic.

▶ Be professional and in control, not too cool or creative.

▶ Be kind, polite and empathetic, never strict or shouty.

▶ Be flexible – don't stick to your plans if they are not working.

The best workshop leaders use influence rather than status because they are there to empower the team to collectively create a way forward, in service of the group.

'Our job is to set the stage, not perform on it'

In a 2014 *Harvard Business Review* article entitled 'Collective genius', Linda Hill and her colleagues lay out three critical aspects of creative leadership:[1]

1 Creative abrasion – creative leaders who can drive debate, inject honesty and amplify differences of opinion within a team to get to a creative outcome.

2 Creative agility – creative leadership that encourages discovery-driven learning, making sure participants test and refine their ideas, and experimenting until the ideas are better.

3 Creative resolution – how creative leaders encourage multiple ideas and diverse perspectives to live alongside each other until the best solutions emerge, rather than conforming or deciding too early on a direction.

As workshop leaders, we need to set up the ingredients for collective genius in the tasks we prepare, the tools we use and the people we invite to participate. Workshops are the ideal space in which the three aspects of creative leadership can be used successfully.

What motivates you to lead?

Here are some common motivations that you might have for wanting to lead, and advice to consider:

Motivation	Advice
Are you an organised person wanting to make your team more organised?	Lead sessions that structure time efficiently but allow people some latitude in how they use that time, so they don't feel your approach is too rigid.
Are you a senior manager who wants your team to take more initiative?	Split up the workshop into sections and have your team (individually or in pairs) run one of the sections of the day, preparing the stimulus, inspiration and leading the workshop under your guidance.
Are you new to a team and have good ideas but unsure of how to influence others?	Ask an experienced team member to work with you to design and lead a workshop for your colleagues to participate in creating ideas with you, so they hear your ideas and contribute their own.
Are you under pressure or overworked, with no time for creativity?	Lead regular, short, well-planned sessions, and rotate the leaders to keep up energy and curiosity despite work pressure.

Motivation	Advice
Are you working on such important issues that it is essential your work reaches people better?	Lead your team in looking outside for inspiration on how to truly engage the people you need to reach.
Are you working in a sick or bureaucratic business culture?	Get permission from your team to test the workshop approach in a time-limited session on an important objective, to show how productive teams can be if they behave in the right way.

How to be a better workshop leader

Use your physical and verbal presence to keep momentum and control in your workshop. It will keep the workshop feeling enjoyable because these are subtle and polite cues that prevent you from having to be strict or serious. They are especially useful to control the time it takes for people to talk in turn, present ideas to each other, or give their observations to the whole group.

Physical

▶ **Organise the room yourself.** This means choosing and setting up the space to work with your design.

▶ **Move around the room** as people speak, so that you are part of the group (standing at the front of the room removes you from the group).

▶ **Move towards people who are speaking** as they talk, giving them encouragement and attention. When you want someone to finish their point, move slowly closer to them, which has the effect of helping them to finish their sentence more quickly.

▶ **Use the hand.** If you are still unable to make someone end their point, once you are very close to them slowly raise your hand, palm towards them, and smile politely – this works well to close off their point and let someone else talk.

Verbal

▶ **Welcome everyone individually** as they arrive at the session, shaking their hand and introducing yourself as the workshop leader.

▶ **Make a clear start.** Make sure everyone is listening and say 'HELLO!' in a loud, clear voice, with a smile. Then pause and wait for people to reply. People smile back when you do this, and most say hello back, too. Thank people for giving up their time to come to the session and explain how important it is that everyone concentrates and participates fully.

▶ **Wait for quiet.** Wait until there is complete silence before giving any instruction, to keep the team clear on what needs to be done and to reinforce your control of the workshop.

▶ **Let people contribute as early as possible.** If you have time and the group is not too large, it is always worth letting them introduce themselves to give everyone a voice at the start of the session, so that they are contributing immediately. I often ask what they would like the workshop to achieve and write down these points to refer to at the end of the workshop, to see if we managed to achieve them.

▶ **Give positive feedback.** When people are sharing ideas, even if you are listening intently, do not stay quiet. Sharing ideas can be scary for the person who is talking, and the workshop leader should be as encouraging as possible with everyone and every idea. Keep giving positive verbal feedback throughout, saying 'yes', 'great idea', 'well done', 'that's good!', etc. This keeps up the momentum as it interrupts monologues and helps people move onto the next point, and it allows you to politely interrupt people when they've talked for too long, with phrases like 'thank you' and 'great' said in a tone of finishing and moving on.

▶ **Reflect on ideas.** A way to make people feel really good about their ideas is to reflect on them, saying something like 'I really like that idea because...' or 'that makes me think of a new idea such as...'

▶ **Be polite.** Keep your tone calm, kind and friendly. Don't shout over the group for any reason.

▶ **Be an example** with your own mood, tone and demeanour. Be confident, calm, positive and energetic, and people will reflect this back to you.

▶ **Listen but don't interfere** in breakout groups. Listen and check in with them to see if they have the information they need and are clear on the task, but don't interfere in breakout discussions unless invited to do so by the team. It can worry people and distract them if they feel they are being watched or interrupted.

► **Don't panic people.** Try not to put people under pressure, even if you do need to keep to time. Instead of saying 'you've got five minutes left!', talk to each group in turn, gently asking if they are ready to move on and explaining there are about five minutes left for this task.

► **Focus your words** on what you want people to do (rather than what you don't want them to do).

► **Give reasons** for each instruction so people understand why they are being asked to do something in a certain way.

► **Close the session** by asking for one comment from each person before they go, for example something they feel has been achieved in the session, or something they are still concerned about. This helps encourage people to share something positive in front of each other (which reminds everyone that they have used their time wisely), but also allows them to express concerns openly (instead of grumbling afterwards).

'Leading effectively is less about mastering situations, or even mastering social skill sets, than about developing a genuine talent for fostering positive feelings in the people whose cooperation and support you need.'

Goleman and Boyatzis

Ask yourself

► Are you committed to helping the team work collaboratively?

► Will you be comfortable allowing the group to define the next steps collectively?

► Do you mind not participating in the breakout groups?

► How can you use your physical and verbal presence to make the workshop feel effortless?

8

CHAPTER EIGHT

Workshop behaviours

The way we behave in groups can improve the quality of ideas we create. If we behave in the same way as we do in everyday meetings, we will come up with the same ideas. Because workshops are an approach to find fresh thinking, it is important to ask people to behave differently to enable the fresh thinking that produces good ideas.

Collective intelligence

Collective intelligence research at MIT identified three factors that correlate with collective intelligence (the ability of a team to come up with better ideas than the most intelligent individual in that team):[1]

1 **Conversational turn takers:** having people in the workshop who are good at listening and speaking in turn, making sure everyone is able to be heard and all views are considered.

2 **Digesters:** having people who are able to digest, understand and empathise with other people's ideas rather than only think about their own.

3 **Women:** a good balance of women in the group helps because they tend to be more likely to take it in turn to speak and listen to others.

Clearly set up behaviours for the participants at the start of every workshop, even if you know the participants are familiar with them already. Explain each behaviour and the reason it is so important.

Behaviour required	Unacceptable behaviour	Reasons why
Create lots and lots of ideas first.	Trying to get to the right idea immediately.	Any idea can lead to new ideas and so creating the wrong idea is not a waste of time. Every idea will be leading us to better ideas.
Assume anything is possible.	Saying an idea will not be possible.	We can't mix creative thinking with evaluation, so don't evaluate the ideas or criticise them until we have created lots. If an idea is not possible, add to it with a better idea that is.
Be constructive and build on other people's ideas.	Being critical about other people's ideas without suggesting better ones.	It's much easier to focus on what's wrong with an idea instead of building on it or improving it. If you don't like an idea you hear, give a better one, or say nothing. Some people will be discouraged when their ideas are criticised and they might not contribute any more.
Write it down.	Intending to say an idea later when you get the chance.	Because we are creating lots of ideas, it's easy to forget some, so be sure to write down any thoughts you have and share them.
Write it again and again until it's right.	Stopping yourself or someone else from writing down an idea because it's not yet perfect.	It is better to write down something immediately and keep adding new versions of it until you are happy. Trying to perfect an idea that does not exist yet stops creative flow.
Don't look for consensus.	Stopping people in the group from writing down an idea until you all agree on it.	We want as many ideas as possible. If you are working in a small team, you don't all need to agree on each idea that's written down. If you have opposite ideas, write both down. This is a spontaneous process, not an evaluative one.
Use 'yes and' and 'how can we...' to build on an idea instead of criticising it.	Saying 'yes but', 'we've tried that before', 'that's too expensive' or 'that will never work'.	In the spirit of being constructive, turn any critical points into constructive questions such as 'how can we make that less expensive?' or 'how can we make that more feasible?', or simply build on an idea by saying 'yes and...'
Be present; don't check phones and laptops.	Checking phones, emails and laptops, or having phones and laptops sitting on the desk during the workshop.	In order to be able to focus properly, we need to be fully present and not multi-tasking. People find it hard to focus on more than one thing at a time. Please feel free to leave the room if you have urgent things to check, but put all phones and laptops out of sight during the workshop.
Use real people's language.	Using technical jargon and company-specific acronyms.	Expressing ideas in normal, everyday language means we are able to get across the meaning behind ideas in a much more straightforward way.

Workshops take us away from the distractions of technology

▶ Research has shown that we get pleasure from novelty,[2] so looking for new messages on our phones and laptops becomes addictive as we get a shot of dopamine, the brain's pleasure chemical, each time we see someone has sent us something new. Because people are addicted, it's hard to make them stop and focus in everyday meetings. Workshops provide a structure and space that help people to focus properly with all their attention.

▶ Neuroscience research has proved that multi-tasking itself does not exist.[3] Scientists measured people who 'multi-tasked' versus those who focused on single subjects. Those who thought they were multi-tasking were in fact doing what is called 'rapid task switching', with lower intelligent output as a result. Our multi-tasking makes everyday meetings less effective, which is why well-planned workshops are vital for making the most of the face-to-face time we do have.

▶ A recent study showed that in some companies people are spending 40 per cent of their time getting through their emails, which means in a five-day week we would start work on a Wednesday.[4] This makes it hard for people to feel comfortable sitting in a meeting without catching up on their emails. One of the main success factors for a workshop is that people are taken away from answering emails and are able to focus and collaborate, without distractions.

Ask yourself

▶ Does the group of people coming to the workshop contain conversational turn takers, digesters and women?

▶ How can we minimise distractions?

▶ Have you clearly set up expectations and behaviours for the day?

▶ Will the people coming give the workshop their full attention?

9

Managing difficult behaviours

How to change difficult behaviour into constructive behaviour

It is quite common to have people in your workshop with 'difficult' behaviours, including not participating, not listening, dominating the group, not being constructive with ideas, refusing to work collaboratively or derailing the workshop in some way that prevents the team from working collectively or prevents the objective being met.

Difficult behaviours may be driven by a dislike of workshops, challenges related to the project, feeling threatened by other members of the team or just being one of those people who is hard to work with, whether in a workshop or not. It is entirely natural for people to have concerns when it comes to workshops, because you are asking people to work in a way that is not within their everyday habits.

By taking away hierarchies and asking for collaboration, people may feel you are taking away their power and status, or the respect they are due, given their expertise. In asking people to do prep tasks, share personal experiences or behave spontaneously with ideas, less confident people get worried about whether they are doing the right thing or are being seen in a good light, and can regret what they reveal about themselves.

The main thing I've learned is to be extra sympathetic to people who have difficulty in workshops, because those behaviours are driven by fear. However, because they can derail your session you must prepare to take extra care to actively plan for and manage difficult behaviours to turn them into constructive behaviours, or the rest of the group will be affected and your workshop will not be successful.

Managing difficult behaviours by understanding the motivations that cause them

Behaviour type	Motivation	How to manage
Clever critic	They want to show their excellent knowledge, grasp of the situation and solutions. Because they are clever and probably better informed than others in the team, they feel they know the answer and so don't see the need to work collaboratively to create it with others.	While it is frustrating to have to manage them, clever critics can be a real help, because they highlight to you early some of the issues or challenges that you might have to face in the project, and it is far better to hear these concerns rather than not be aware of them. Spend time with them in advance, so they have contributed their clever thoughts and don't feel the need to criticise as much during the workshop. If possible, ask them to run a section of the workshop that you work on together, so they feel they've had their chance to influence.
Exasperated expert	They've been in a job for a long time and feel that nobody ever listens to them. They have seen lots of projects come and go, and nothing ever seems to get done. They feel their time and expertise are being wasted.	Find a way of giving them a prominent voice within the session, perhaps by running a small section or giving a presentation so they feel they have been heard.
Terrified to talk	They are shy, worried they will say the wrong thing, don't feel qualified to be in the workshop, or speak a different language. They might prefer to consider carefully what to say before speaking.	Warn people in advance about the types of questions you will ask them, so they feel ready to answer. Ask everyone to write answers on Post-its before they talk and hand them in as they make their point. This makes sure that the less confident people will still be heard, even if the dominant people speak first. Working in small groups makes introverts feel safer. Allow teams to work in first-language groups with each other, or with translation, rather than in English.
Repressed creative	They want to show a different side of themselves to their team members, to prove how talented and creative they are beyond their current job.	Allow them some time to show their creativity, perhaps by preparing a small section for them to prepare and present. Be careful to keep them focused on the objective, as they risk being fixed on the creativity over the outputs.

Behaviour type	Motivation	How to manage
Reluctant participant	They are pessimistic about what can be achieved so don't want to waste their time investing effort in something that won't work. They may have had bad experiences of workshops in the past.	Recognise their concerns and voice them in the workshop so they know you are aware of these concerns (for example, 'I know you've been in several workshops on this topic – here's how we will run this one differently'). Recognise their reluctance and provide positive reinforcement. Remind them of their role in making the workshop a success.
Passive aggressive	They want to challenge the workshop leader's authority without appearing to do so, usually because they feel threatened or don't want to lose status.	Immediately stop them from taking the workshop off track by reiterating what you have asked. Reinforce the reasons why the instruction is important and don't let them abstain from full participation.
Superior being	They are important, and their job is important. They might not have time to attend but want to be there and so try to multi-task by attending but not participating.	Talk to senior people in advance about your expectations for full participation by every attendee. Ask everyone to check phones and emails outside the room. Explain how valuable the time of each person here is and talk about the importance of respect. Welcome open challenges.
Ideas bully	They want to prove they know better, to make other people look bad and their ideas win.	Explain the rules and behaviours, and if they continue to bully, isolate them in pairs with someone strong, or someone else difficult, or take them aside (or ask your stakeholder to do so) and ask them to behave.

Turning difficult behaviour into constructive behaviour

If you know that a person will not be able to change their behaviour from difficult to constructive, try not to have them in your workshop. Explain to them in advance the behaviours required and gently point out that they might not be a good fit for the session, but can input ideas beforehand and help with the decisions afterwards. Unfortunately, it is often the people with difficult behaviours that need to be there, because if they are not part of it they will be even more difficult to manage later on.

Here are some ways to change difficult behaviours into constructive behaviours:

▶ Meet with the person before the workshop to explain the behaviours and the plan, so that they can express concerns early, rather than on the day.

▶ Be very specific about what you expect them to change in their behaviours – don't just hint at it. Sometimes difficult people are not aware of the impact of their behaviours. Use real examples to help them understand what you mean, and make very clear what is and is not acceptable.

▶ Help people by constructing their language for them. Instead of asking 'what is wrong with this idea?', ask them 'what improvements can you suggest to make this idea better?'. Or if they suggest a negative point, ask them to turn that point into an idea, suggestion or improvement. You will need to do this several times before they get used to it.

▶ Have a reward or penalty system (if appropriate to the team). For a more creative team you can have something funny like a rubber chicken of punishment that gets given to anyone who is not being constructive – this is a good way to get your team to help you control behaviours because they can pass the chicken to each other with a bit of a laugh, while still making a clear point. For more serious teams you could have a yellow card, red card system, and enforce a meaningful but light penalty for receiving a red card, for example be silent for 10 minutes, make tea for everyone in the room or put some money in a donation jar for charity.

▶ Give them a constructive role within the workshop, such as running one section, or specify a time when they can be as critical as they like, but only after the initial ideas are created.

▶ Have different people at the workshop, for example customers or experts. People tend to behave better in front of strangers than they do in front of familiar people.

▶ Use structured templates with clear instructions, so there are fewer questions and fewer chances to go off track.

Ask yourself

▶ Who is likely to be difficult and why?

▶ Do you feel you will be able to stay in control during the workshop?

▶ What strategies will you use to get people to listen to you?

▶ What rewards and penalties will work well with this group?

▶ Is there anyone you can ask not to attend?

10

The workshop energy

'I've learned that people will forget what you said, people will forget what you did, but people will never forget how you made them feel.'

Maya Angelou

Workshops put pressure on people to behave well, come up with new ideas and stay focused. Workshops can be tiring, especially after lunch and near the end of the day.

The workshop leader can make the experience energetic and inspiring throughout with some of these simple approaches:

▶ **Move people into new groups** after each ideas session. Sitting in new teams at a new table immediately gives a fresh perspective and instils energy.

▶ **Be positive and energetic**, modelling the mood you want the workshop participants to have.

▶ **Keep calm**; be careful not to shout, rush or stress people out too much or they will lose the energy to participate.

▶ **Have different people speak**, whether that be your stakeholder at the beginning of the day, a guest speaker or a co-facilitator or handing over one section to a different team member to lead.

▶ **Use food and drink** as part of your workshop design. We ran a workshop in Germany that included a 'pimp my pasta' lunch where groups cooked pasta together using various ingredients, then we voted on the best pasta dish and ate together. The exercise created starting points for new reality entertainment ideas.

▶ **Have regular breaks** with healthy food and snacks and some treats.

▶ **Change the room during the lunch break**, so that it feels like a new space when the participants come back.

▶ **Tidy away clutter** such as empty cups and old Post-its all day.

▶ **Have time limits** for tasks to prevent people getting bored. This is a balance, because you don't want people to feel rushed, but giving too much time saps energy.

▶ **Mix up the tasks.** Even if the end deliverable is the same (for example, an ideas sheet), make the techniques and tasks feel different, so that the participants are always learning how to perform to a new set of instructions.

▶ **Play music.** Music is a powerful tool for creating the desired mood, to lift the mood at the beginning, calm the mood in a more reflective session or provide background noise when teams are sitting close to each other but don't want to be overheard.

▶ **Give gifts and prizes.** Make people feel special and encouraged to pay more attention by spiking their energy levels with competitions and rewards. Giving people the chance to win small prizes that they can eat, drink or take away with them will make people engage with the activity more, and form positive associations overall.

▶ **Use multi-sensory boxes.** Create a selection of boxes to bring to life a customer need, a theme or area, or a type of person. Inside the boxes have a rich mixture of carefully chosen items that can be unpacked, unwrapped, tasted, touched, smelled, drunk and eaten. Each item serves as a stimulus for new ideas, and just the excitement of the unpacking is an energiser in itself. It also creates energy and bonds the group as they are exploring something new together.

Using energiser games

I rarely use energiser games – I find I can keep energy levels high without them. However, some teams want to have fun with each other and playing a quick game can give everyone a little break between sessions. Laughter is good for ideas too, so the more fun the better. Be careful not to cause any embarrassment or inappropriateness (I remember a friend of mine telling me how in one energiser she found herself sitting on her boss's lap). I'm very careful about how and when to use energisers, and usually do so only when I know the team very well.

Ask yourself

▶ Would you enjoy participating in this workshop?

▶ Have you considered ways to create and maintain energy?

▶ How can you make this an even more effortless and enjoyable session?

▶ Have you surprised and delighted the workshop participants in some way?

▶ Have you made this workshop feel different from other workshops they might have been to in the past?

Action

Putting workshops into action

Action pulls together the Design and Lead principles into workshop plans. Each chapter in this part of the book is based on a type of workshop objective, with tools and an example session plan for your reference. These outlines should guide you to create your own versions of tools and plans to suit your workshop objective.

11

Basic workshop tools

Use for: helping people to create fresh ideas in any workshop

When we are good at our jobs, the experience we have built up over time means that we take in relevant information and make decisions faster. Unfortunately, these habits prevent us from coming up with new thinking and fresh ideas.

The workshop objective: to create new angles from which to look at problems, using workshop tools

These new angles help people think in non-rational and non-linear ways, to avoid their brains from following the same habits of thinking. They help even very experienced people to look at the same old problem from a fresh angle.

'Every child is an artist, the problem is staying an artist when you grow up.'

Pablo Picasso

Consider a one-year-old child who has not yet formed many habits. If a one year old sees a shoe, for example, they might think it's a hat, or a boat to play with in the bath, or something to chew on. Over time the child learns that the shoe goes on her foot, and that association gets stronger and stronger as it is repeated so that she can get dressed in the morning without too much fuss.

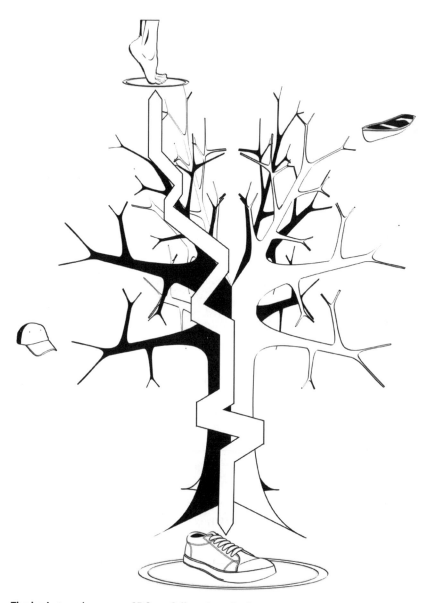

The brain tree (see page 65 for a full explanation)

The same thing happens at work. We get better at our jobs by repeating the same associations and ideas, and the pathways we use to do this become stronger and help us make faster decisions.[1] This is great for our jobs because those patterns build our ability to deal with the same experience successfully in future. However, it also means that people find it hard to see new ways of approaching problems, particularly if they are very experienced at their job or have worked in the same way for a long time.

Why we need workshop tools

Workshop tools are like a holiday for the brain. They take people away from the objective or problem, then give a fresh perspective when that objective is re-visited. Workshop tools create fresh and relevant angles.

As the workshop leader, consider how to structure your session in a way that helps the team to look at the problem from new angles. There are many tools that can be used within a workshop in order to encourage people to be more creative. Here are some examples of the tools I use regularly.

Magazine cut-outs

▶ Buy lots of magazines related to your topic or customer.

▶ Ask people to cut out any headlines, words, themes or pictures that leap out at them, very spontaneously.

▶ Then ask the team to group the cut-outs on some flipchart paper, creating some common themes.

▶ Split the team into smaller groups, each taking one theme, and use that theme and the words and images within it to inspire some new ideas for the objective.

Top tunes

▶ Prepare a playlist of songs that relate to your topic or customer.

▶ Play one song after the other while people listen and write down any words, phrases, memories or emotions that occur to them during the songs.

▶ Split the team into pairs and ask them to share their notes with each other and use the notes to create new ideas.

Bookstore brainstorm

▶ Take your workshop to a big bookstore.

▶ Allow the team to explore the bookstore for 30 minutes with the workshop objective in mind, taking notes or photos of relevant language, titles or other information that relates to the topic in some way.

▶ Put the team into small groups to share their notes and photos and use these to create some new ideas.

Letter ladder

▶ Seat the team in a circle, giving them each a blank sheet of paper.

▶ Ask them to write down five words associated with the topic down the left-hand side of the paper.

▶ Each person passes their paper clockwise.

▶ With the new sheets, each person uses the words written on the left-hand side to trigger some new ideas or angles which they write down in the right-hand column.

▶ Get the team into pairs and ask them to share their sheets, angles and ideas, and use these to create some new ideas.

Fresh eyes

▶ Prepare either a list of well-known personalities or a list of successful organisations that relate to your topic in some way.

▶ Split the team into groups of three and ask them to choose one personality or organisation to work on.

▶ Ask each team to consider how this personality or organisation would approach our topic area, listing at least 10 different points for how they might do so.

▶ Use those 10 points as inspiration for new ideas on the topic.

Planning to use workshop tools

Using workshop tools involves three stages. All the exercises and session plans in this book follow this pattern. As a workshop leader, separate the instructions to your team per stage. Give just the instructions for each stage, one at a time, before giving the next, as follows:

Stage and leader's instruction	Explanation for this stage
1 Now we are going to put the workshop objective out of mind for a bit while we do a small task.	This is to give you some new angles to think from. Don't be worried about the end goal at this point.
2 Give the instructions for the tool, so that the team create new angles, none of which needs to make sense for the topic yet.	This is about generating a wealth of new angles to choose from – the more you create, the more possibilities you have for inspiring new ideas.
3 Use the new angles as inspiration for new ideas that relate back to the workshop objective. Focus on the ones that give you new thoughts and create some ideas for those. Choose some absurd angles as well as some obvious ones to generate ideas from.	Now use the new angles to look at the topic from a new perspective, even if absurd, in order to disrupt your brain habits and create unusual and innovative ideas.

Putting the tools together into a workshop plan

Plan to cover several rounds of generating ideas in your workshop. If you have only one hour, then one round is fine, but if you can apply at least a couple of tools to the topic, you will find that the quality and volume of ideas are better because they've been approached from a few angles and not just one.

An easy way to plan your session is to identify three possible idea directions to focus the ideas on. For example:

▶ three different target customers to consider (e.g. child, parent, grandparent)

▶ three different product issues to solve (packaging, formulation, storage)

▶ three parts of the business to improve (front of house, shopfloor staff, loading bay)

▶ three different contact points with the end user (helpline, website, in store)

▶ three points in time we need to consider (past, present, future)

▶ three values we believe are important (transparency, efficiency, quality).

Then, for each of these three topics, use a different workshop tool to bring fresh thinking to that particular topic. Finally, consider what kinds of ideas you want out of each round. Putting these together in a plan would look like this:

Introduction and objectives		
Direction A	Workshop tool 1	Ideas round 1
Direction B	Workshop tool 2	Ideas round 2
Direction C	Workshop tool 3	Ideas round 3
Prioritise and next steps		

Session plan

Example of using fresh angles for new ideas

If you were a shoe company looking for new shoe ideas, you'd find it hard to look beyond the shoe–foot association. Instead, if we approached the topic from a new angle, as a one-year-old child might, we could take each new angle and use it to inspire new shoe ideas, as follows:

Using 'hat' to inspire new shoe ideas:

▶ because it protects from the sun, ideas for shoes that contain UV sensors to warn you about sun damage on your run

▶ leading to an idea about vitamin- or energy-infused pouches that refresh the muscles in your feet over a long run

▶ leading to caffeine-infused shoes that give you energy while you run

▶ leading to shoes you put on after your run or a long day on your feet, to revive and comfort them.

Using 'boat' to inspire new shoe ideas:

▶ because it is about water, shoes that are both breathable and waterproof, letting moisture out, not in, during sport

▶ leading to shoes for boating and sailing that dry fast after being in water

▶ leading to shoes that help you walk on water by displacing puddles and rain as you walk through them with a mild hydrophobic action.

Using 'something to chew on' to inspire new shoe ideas:

▶ because it's about food and energy, shoes that contain a kinetic action that is driven by movement, so that you can charge your phone or generate energy based on the amount your feet move

▶ leading to an idea of measuring the movement of thousands of people who commit to exercising more, using sensors in their shoes that are linked to discounts in their health insurance premiums.

Ask yourself

▶ Have you thought about how to create new angles before creating ideas?

▶ What tools will help you create the right sort of ideas?

▶ Have you prepared several different rounds of ideas?

12

Bringing a topic to life

Use for: bringing something to life so that people feel and live it rather than just hear about it

Bringing a topic to life means giving people a way of living and feeling the topic, instead of just listening to a series of presentations.

The workshop objective: to help people physically and emotionally engage with the topic

Because we want to inspire fresh thinking, consider fresh approaches to giving people information. Making people feel something is an effective way of inspiring ideas, so think about how to grab people's attention by raising their personal experience of the topic.

There are many ways to bring information to life in a workshop, for example:

▶ **Create a short film** or animation to tell the story.

▶ **Use diagrams, posters and photographs** that people can explore at their own pace. For example, on a food project, we had a panel of foodies take pictures of their kitchen, their products and their mealtimes for a week. That way the team saw their customers not just as a series of statistics but in pictures with their families, their houses and in their actual kitchens. This led them to consider packaging ideas that would allow their product to be displayed on the counter, rather than put away in a cupboard.

▶ **Choose an inspiring meeting space** that does the job for you. For example, we ran a sustainability workshop at a city farm and the sounds and smells of the animals were far more evocative than a glass meeting room would have been.

▶ **Create a multi-sensory experience** by getting people to go out and see, hear, feel and smell the topic first hand. For example, for a project on stock cubes, we took the team to a secret supper at a customer's house for their evening meal to give them insights into how everyday people were taking pleasure and pride in serving sophisticated food.

▶ **Talk to someone extreme.** Rather than only from talking to target customers, ideas can come from the fringes and edges of your target. For example, on a project on digital behaviours, we sent people to spend the day with an extreme technology addict and also with someone who was a complete technophobe, to see what motivations they both had and what fears they were facing when it came to the digital world.

A cultural experience example

I ran a series of workshops for a global team working on deodorants. We wanted to inspire ideas by giving them first-hand experience of each of their main consumers, countries and sweat-producing activities.

Here are just a few examples of the many activities we prepared for those workshops:

▶ Debating definitions of masculinity with young Nigerian men in London.

▶ Hearing an anthropologist talking about purity and dirt in Indian culture.

▶ Ethnographic films from Russian, Nigerian and Brazilian homes.

▶ Participating in a Russian ballet, Brazilian capoeira or American line dancing lesson.

▶ Competing in a treasure hunt in 40-degree heat in Buenos Aires.

▶ Playing indoor cricket with Brits and Australians in New York.

▶ Having a yoga lesson before an Indian breakfast.

The team members then had structured creative discussions to combine their personal experiences with conversations with the consumers. One of the marketing directors said it was the best day at work she had ever had in her career, because she had a chance to experience the activities herself, rather than just being presented to. As well as achieving the business objective, doing a range of activities together was a great team-building experience.

Ask yourself

▶ How can you bring your workshop topic to life?

▶ How much can you make people actively do instead of listening to?

▶ How can you inspire people?

▶ What senses can you ignite?

13

Creating quick ideas

> **Use for:** creating a set of quick ideas in a short space of time
>
> If you don't have a lot of time to prepare, or you plan on running a very quick session, you can design a basic workshop plan and lead it well to get quality ideas. Quick ideas sessions can be fun because you don't have any of the challenges of a long workshop, such as keeping the energy up or stopping people getting bored. Even for a quick session, however, you will still need to invest some time in preparation.

> **The workshop objective:** to create quick, quality ideas in a short space of time
>
> The key to a quick ideas session is to use most of the time for creative (divergent) thinking and do evaluative (convergent) thinking afterwards.

Creative thinking is best done in a group, with all the energy, stimulus and momentum that comes from collaborating.[1] Evaluation can be done individually or by a small group and shared more widely for comment.

This means that if you have only an hour, you should spend it on two or three rounds of idea-generation sessions, getting out the most divergent thinking, and save the evaluation and convergent thinking for later.

What makes people creative

There is a temptation to label an individual 'creative' rather than calling the process the individual might undertake 'creative'.[2] Of course, some people find being creative easier than others. Creativity, however, is something that happens beyond the individual level. Research into successful artists, scientists and entrepreneurs shows that creativity happens only when people combine their personal perspective with their field of expertise in response to a cultural context.[3]

There are three ingredients that make creativity happen:

▶ **Personal experience:** the individual who brings their unique personal talent and perspective to the topic (including family background, personality traits, social circumstances).

▶ **Field of expertise:** the domain and body of knowledge in which the individual is working to create the ideas (the business they work in, their area of expertise, their role in the team, the organisation they belong to).

▶ **Cultural context:** the cultural context in which the individual and domain sit (the society they live in, the economics and demographics happening at this time, the trends that people are affected by).

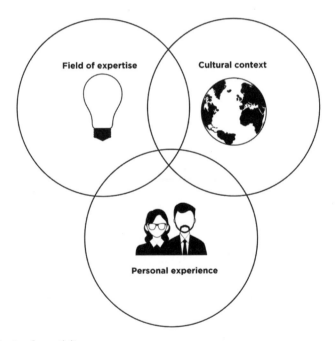

Ingredients of creativity

Often when people try to create new ideas they tend to focus on their field of expertise – what they already know, the area of business they work in, what they have done already – and use that to inspire the answer. However, to make the conditions right for creativity, workshop leaders must enhance the *personal experience* of every individual in the room, as well as the inspiration offered by bringing in the *cultural context* of the topic, in addition to referring to the *field of expertise*.

Prep tasks for participants

A good way to enhance both personal experience and the cultural context for your workshop is to ask each person attending to do a prep task.

If you walk into the room with the same people and look at the same information, you will come up with the same answers. As well as inviting different people to participate, be sure to bring fresh information to inspire the team that brings in culture, personal experience and their expertise at work.

Always ask the participants themselves to help with the stimulus via some prep tasks, for example:

▶ **Personal experience:** ask people to bring an example of a product, service or experience they have recently had and be prepared to talk about it (this should be related to the topic, so for example if your workshop is about improving customer service, ask them to bring an example of when they have personally had a wonderful or terrible customer service experience).

▶ **Field of expertise:** ask people to look at their expertise from a new angle (for example, explain a technology as if explaining it to a child, or look at the competition and what they are doing – anything that takes us beyond the obvious information we usually look at).

▶ **Cultural context:** invite people to bring an example that represents a trend or cultural phenomenon of the time, either a small fad or a big movement, and be prepared to talk about what they think are the reasons for its existence.

The story of Paraffin Young[4]

My great-great-great-grandfather was James Young, who invented the process by which paraffin was distilled from coal into a solid wax. Young patented this process in 1850 and became one of the most famous Scotsmen of his time. He was nicknamed 'Paraffin Young' and went on to sponsor his friend David Livingstone to explore Africa.

Young was not born a creative genius. He was an apprentice joiner while he studied at night school before becoming the assistant to a chemistry lecturer, Thomas Graham. He then embarked on his own career in chemistry. When working in an oil mine, he noticed that oil was dripping from the sandstone roof. This observation led him to develop the distillation method by which paraffin was extracted from coal. ▶

▶ **Personal experience:** Young had a wide range of experience, creating a large variety of ideas beyond chemistry and coal for most of his early life. He was an entrepreneurial and inventive talent.

▶ **Field of expertise:** Young was surrounded by mentors, experts and other inventors, such as Thomas Graham, who began early work into the technology now used in kidney dialysis. Young had worked for years to build his knowledge of coal and natural petroleum before inventing paraffin.

▶ **Cultural context:** Young lived at a time when scientific advances were moving at an unprecedented rate. The time was right for new ideas and patents, and he happened to make the most of that context to create a product that is still used around the world today.

The same kind of story can be told about Mozart, whose personal talent was enhanced by the other musicians who inspired him, the patrons who supported him and the times he lived in.

'Creativity isn't about making things, it's about making things happen.'

Tanner Christensen

Theming tool

The theming tool is an easy and effective tool I use in every workshop. It is simply grouping together ideas by having them written on separate Post-its, which can then be moved and put into themes. These visual themes become new angles for people to focus on. Theming is a perfect tool to use to turn prep tasks into stimuli ready to use in the session.

How to theme

1 Ask participants to individually write down on individual Post-its any thoughts and ideas they have in response to a question.

2 Collect the Post-its and sort them into themes.

3 Split the participants into smaller teams, giving each team one theme to use for inspiration for new ideas.

Why theming works

▶ Theming disrupts linear patterns of writing and thought. Reordering the thoughts and ideas encourages you to look for patterns.

▶ Theming shows what the most popular idea or thought is, rather like a visual form of voting. So, for example, if one theme has 20 Post-its and the other has 3, the theme with 20 is obviously more relevant to the workshop team and should be a main focus.

▶ It ensures that even the most timid members of the workshop have contributed to the thinking, and shows everyone that their thoughts are represented.

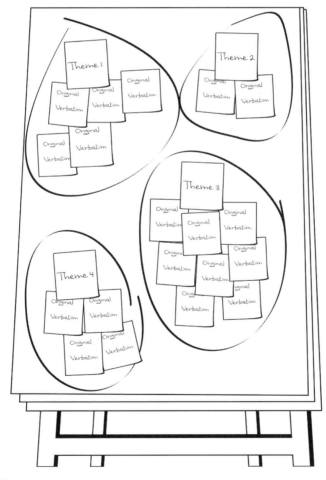

Theming

Quick ideas workshop plan (1.5-hour workshop)

Time	Task
09.00	▶ Welcome + objective + reminder of creative behaviours
09.10	▶ Participants introduce themselves with prep task 1 (bring an example of a product, service or experience they have recently had and be prepared to talk about it)
	▶ They each write three separate Post-its about why they chose that example and hand these to the workshop leader
09.30	▶ Workshop leader themes the Post-its into groups and splits the team into groups of three
	▶ Each group is given one theme from prep task 1 and they use the Post-its within that theme as new angles to give them three new ideas
	▶ Each group presents their ideas back
09.50	▶ Workshop leader splits team into pairs, making sure everyone works with someone new
	▶ Ask each pair to share with each other prep task 2 (look at their expertise from a new angle), making notes and discussing each other's information
	▶ Each pair uses the discussion to create three new ideas inspired by prep task 2
	▶ Each group presents their ideas back
10.10	▶ Workshop leader splits team into new groups of three, making sure everyone works with someone new for this last round
	▶ Ask each group to share with each other prep task 3 (bring an example of a trend or cultural phenomenon), making notes and discussing each other's information
	▶ Each group uses the discussion to create three new ideas inspired by prep task 3
	▶ Each group presents their ideas back
10.25	▶ Workshop leader reminds the team of the workshop objective and criteria for choosing next steps
	▶ Team vote on their favourite ideas/idea themes to develop further
	▶ Closing comments from each team member
10.30	▶ Workshop ends

Ask yourself

▶ How can we get inspiration from the outside world into this session?

▶ What are other people and organisations out there doing, and can this inspire us?

▶ Do we know what our customers and consumers are thinking and wanting?

▶ Do we have the right experts or fresh thinkers in the workshop to help us have more ideas?

▶ How can we learn from the unique and personal perspective of each individual in the room?

14

Creating ideas that build on past successes

'It is only in our willingness to persist in the face of fear, judgment and the unknown… that we give opportunity for our creative and innovative ideas to be realized.'

Jonathan Fields

Use for: looking to the past to inspire new ideas

If you are leading a workshop that builds on past successes, be careful to design inspiration that goes beyond what has always been done. People find it easy to shy away from doing something new in case it doesn't work and lean towards doing something that has been done before. New ideas and directions can build on past successes, but people need to have an eye on the future and consider how to maintain that success.

The workshop objective: to inspire ambitious ideas based on past success

One of the biggest temptations in workshops like this is that people look inwards, reflecting only on their own organisation, team or people. With this type of objective, encourage your team to look outside for past successes, at your competitors and at other industries that have succeeded.

People also prefer to look at successes rather than discussing failure, because talking about failure is uncomfortable. As well as defining success and how it comes about, consider failures and what they can teach us.

Do	Don't
Make sure company heroes and successful projects are championed, focusing on the reasons why they were successful rather than the team or project itself – these reasons will be the inspiration for new ideas.	Assume the internal narrative about the project is correct – question why the project was a success, look for unsung heroes of that project, look for luck and influencers of that success that were beyond the project team's actions.
Look beyond your team, project or organisation for examples of success. Consider competitors, other markets and non-competitive products and services that your customers also use.	Look internally for inspiration only.
Consider failures – internal, with competitors and in the wider industry for your customer – being sure to identify the reasons for failure and calibrating them against the reasons for success (often they will match each other).	Focus on the failure per se. Focus on the ways of working, circumstances and attitudes that led to that failure.

Idea stretcher tool

When you are building on past successes, there is a temptation to create safe ideas because you have ways of working that are successful and therefore teams tend not to stretch themselves. In situations like this you need to help teams go beyond the obvious and into the extreme to make sure they are being as ambitious with their thinking as possible.

The idea stretcher tool is a great way to take the obvious, stretch it out, then bring it back into the realms of the realistic. Please note that the order of filling in each column is important – they are not just left to right.

How to use it

1 Column A: write four success factors in the boxes on the left-hand side. For example:

  ▶ We have one main product that everyone recognises

2 Column B: for each of the success factors, stretch it to a completely extreme version of that idea. For example:

  ▶ We have 100 products that everyone recognises

3 Column C: work the extreme version down to something innovative. For example:

  ▶ We have 100 versions of our main product

4 Column D: Then work the innovative idea into something ambitious yet possible. For example:

   ▶ We create a product range with some more modern versions of our main product, to keep customers happy and attract new customers with our new versions

5 Repeat the exercise for the other three ideas.

6 The completed template gives you some angles for new ideas – either by choosing the ambitious ideas or by taking inspiration from any other angles on the sheet.

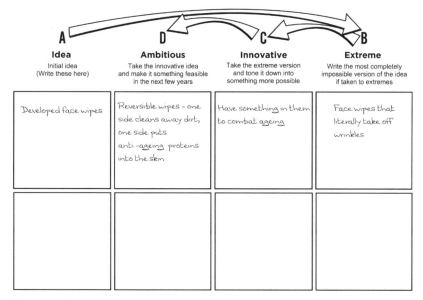

Idea stretcher

The idea stretcher is good for:

▶ ideas, claims, ways of working or initiatives that run the risk of being obvious or unambitious

▶ teams who think in a rational manner and are concerned about going too far

▶ allowing otherwise cautious people to safely push ideas beyond the possible, then bring them back to the safe and feasible

▶ structuring more ambitious thinking.

Mini case study tool

It is important for team members to take inspiration from other companies, industries and organisations beyond their own, even if they have been successful thus far. A good way to structure this inspiration is by preparing mini case study cards, which are a set of 5–10 short case studies about companies, organisations or brands that you as the workshop leader feel will inspire the team.

When choosing these, I tend to try for some unusual examples, rather than the usual suspects like Apple, Facebook or Google. For example:

▶ For toothpaste ideas we used case studies about repair, from ceramic repairers to bicycle puncture kits.

▶ For ways of working ideas for a team of IT specialists, we used examples of customer service from Amazon, Harrods and Virgin Atlantic.

▶ For shampoo ideas we found case studies on cosmetics, dog grooming and health food.

Prepare your case studies in advance, with some imagery of their branding, pictures of their store or people, and a short description of their work and what they do. Make sure the brands are diverse – try to include a range of different product or service types, a range of customers, and some huge companies as well as some local hero brands or charities.

How to use the mini case study tool

1 Split the team into small groups.

2 Ask each group to choose one brand case study to work on (so that every team is working on something different). For example: 'Come Dine With Me' (TV show).

3 In small groups, list at least 10 reasons why that brand, product or company is successful. For the 'Come Dine With Me' example, some of the reasons we enjoy watching it are:

▶ We love to look inside other people's houses.

▶ It's a way of experiencing a dinner party without having to have one yourself.

▶ It's a chance to judge other people's cooking, so it makes me feel better about my own cooking.

4 Teams then use those reasons as new angles for ideas, focusing on each of the reasons in turn to see if they inspire any new ideas. For example, if we were to use 'Come Dine With Me' to inspire new ideas for a restaurant:

▶ We love to look inside other people's houses – could lead to an idea for a 'Dinner Party' restaurant that feels like someone's actual home (split into four unique kitchen + living room + dining room combinations in a range of interior design styles, from casual to formal). You would book your choice of room combinations, discuss your evening and menu with a personal chef, invite your guests to attend, then work on the menu and cook the meal with your chef helping and advising you.

▶ It's a way of experiencing a dinner party without having to have one yourself – could lead to an idea for a restaurant where you invite friends to work with the chef in advance to design one unique course for the table, so one person designs the aperitif, the next the starter, another person the main course and finally dessert and cheese. The group dining together feel they have created a menu without needing to cook it themselves or clean up afterwards.

▶ It's a chance to judge other people's cooking, so it makes me feel better about my own cooking – could lead to an idea of a restaurant that sends people home after a meal with the ingredients and instructions for how to make that meal at home.

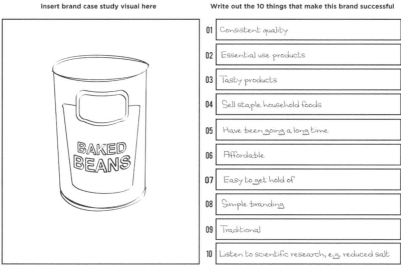

Insert brand case study visual here   Write out the 10 things that make this brand successful

01	Consistent quality
02	Essential use products
03	Tasty products
04	Sell staple household foods
05	Have been going a long time
06	Affordable
07	Easy to get hold of
08	Simple branding
09	Traditional
10	Listen to scientific research, e.g. reduced salt

Mini case study

Building on past successes workshop plan (4-hour workshop)

Time	Task
09.00	▶ Welcome + objective + reminder of creative behaviours
09.10	▶ Participants introduce themselves with a prep task (bring an example of a product, service or experience they have recently had and be prepared to talk about it) ▶ They each write three separate Post-its about why they chose that example and hand these to the workshop leader
09.30	▶ Workshop leader themes the Post-its into groups and splits the team into groups of three ▶ Each group is given one theme from prep task 1 and they use the Post-its within that theme as new angles to give them three new ideas ▶ Each group presents their ideas back
10.00	▶ Workshop leader splits team into pairs, making sure everyone works with someone new ▶ Ask each pair to choose one mini case study and write out 10 reasons why that brand, product or service is successful ▶ Each pair uses the 10 reasons as new angles to create three new ideas inspired by the case studies ▶ Each group presents their ideas back
11.00	▶ Break
11.15	▶ Workshop leader splits team into new groups of three, making sure everyone works with someone new for this last round ▶ Give each group an idea stretcher template, asking them to write down their four reasons for past success, then the obvious new ideas from that, before filling in the completely mad and finally innovative and ambitious ▶ Each group uses the completed template as inspiration to create three new ideas inspired by prep task 3 ▶ Each group presents their ideas back
12.15	▶ Workshop leader reminds the team of the workshop objective and criteria for choosing next steps ▶ Team vote on their favourite ideas/idea themes to develop further
12.30	▶ Workshop leader splits the team into new groups of three, with each group taking one of the best ideas or themes to develop into actions and next steps ▶ Closing comments from each team member
13.00	▶ Workshop ends

Ask yourself

▶ Have you encouraged the attendees to take inspiration from other companies, industries and organisations beyond their own?

▶ Have you organised a way to bring outside inspiration in?

▶ Have you made sure the ideas will be stretched, not safe?

▶ Have you focused on the reasons why the idea was successful as opposed to the idea itself?

15

CHAPTER FIFTEEN

Improving existing ideas

Use for: making sure you don't lose the essence of good ideas when you improve them

Ideas build on each other. Every idea is made up of the many ideas that preceded it. If there are ideas that already exist that need improving, be careful not to throw away all the work that has been done to get there. It is easier to create completely new ideas than improve the existing ones, because we tend to want to create our own ideas, instead of improving on the work of others.

The workshop objective: to improve ideas by building on their strengths

When a new set of people look at an idea for the first time, they tend to come at it from a very critical mind set. Because they didn't create it, it is easy to work out what is wrong with it. The risk of this is that they change the idea beyond recognition when they try to improve it.

The most important thing to do before you begin to improve existing ideas is to identify the strengths of the idea and the essence of the idea that must not be lost, before working out what needs to be improved. The essence of the idea (the core benefit) is different from the execution of it (how it might be made to deliver that benefit).

The difference between essence and execution

I was doing a workshop on innovating fragrance sprays for the toilet. We had found a product need: that people who use them want to spray after they have been to the toilet, but don't want the spray mist to fall on them. So people were spraying and rushing out of the room quickly before the fragrance settled. This led to an idea for an electric unit inside the toilet with a timer that would spray the toilet after the person left the room.

When we reached the stage of voting on ideas, the technical leader in the team did not want us to include the idea in the list of final ideas to develop, even though it had the most votes. When I asked him why, he said it wasn't feasible because it would mean putting power supplies in toilets and might be dangerous in a bathroom. In my mind, using the electricity supply was just one possible execution of the idea.

The essence of the idea was that the spray was timed for just after the person left the room. Whether the concept used a mechanical timer that went off when the door was closed or a button you pressed before you left the room that delayed the spray for five minutes, there were many possible executions of that idea that would be more feasible and keep the essence of the core benefit.

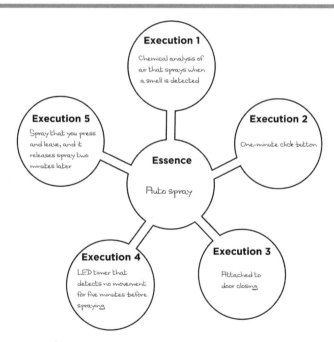

Essence vs execution

Identifying the essence

One of the most important things that you need to do before you improve ideas is to make sure you identify what the essence of the idea is and therefore what benefits must not be lost when improving it.

Keep or grow tool

This tool helps to identify the essence of an idea as well as to work out what needs to be developed before any work is done to improve the idea.

1 Take existing ideas and stick them up around the room.

2 Below each idea put up a flipchart which has 'keep' on one side and 'grow' on the other side.

3 Ask people to read each idea in turn, writing down as many keep Post-its as they can, using the 'keep' statements to help keep the wording of each point constructive.

4 Once all the 'keeps' are written, move onto writing down what can be improved or developed in the 'grow' section, using the wording suggested to keep sentences constructive.

5 You can then split the team into groups and ask each group to take one idea, with all the 'keeps' and 'grows', back to their table.

6 Ask each group to theme the Post-its under 'keep' and 'grow' and from those themes identify what must be kept (what is the essence and main benefit of the idea), before then identifying how to focus on what to grow (any improvements that need to be made).

7 At this point, teams can then begin to work on improving the ideas.

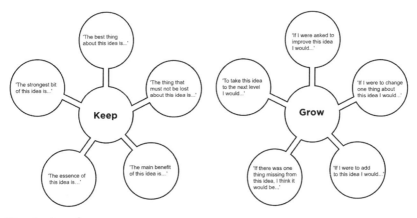

'Keep' or 'grow'

Ideas measure tool

The ideas measure tool can be used to assess ideas, measure their strengths and weaknesses, and identify what to work on to improve them.

1 Plot the ideas down the left-hand column of the template.

2 Along the top row write in the important criteria that the idea will be measured on, for example fits with brand, meets consumer needs, is innovative, is sustainable, is better than competitors, etc.

3 Ask participants to work on each idea in turn, horizontally, using a tick, dash, line or question mark, before moving on to the next idea.

4 Once all the ideas are complete, the team have created a visual map of the strengths of each idea and where each idea needs to be improved on.

5 Then you can send away the different teams to work on improving the weaknesses of each idea.

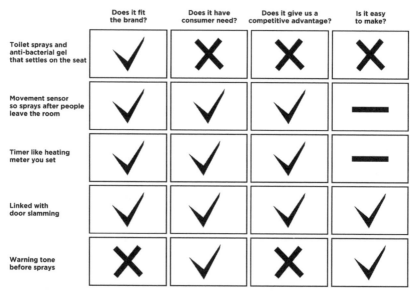

Ideas measure tool

Note: instead of ticks and crosses, you could use a traffic light system (green = strong, orange = OK and red = weak) or a three-point system that can be added into overall scores (1 = poor, 2 = average, 3 = good).

Improving ideas workshop plan (4-hour workshop)

Time	Task
09.00	▶ Welcome + objective + reminder of creative behaviours
09.15	▶ Present original ideas which they will be working on today
09.30	▶ Ask each group to use the 'keep' or 'grow' tool ▶ Groups improve the ideas based on the keep/grow guidelines and present back the improved ideas to the teams
10.15	▶ Split into teams to define the essence of each idea and the improvements to be made to it
10.45	▶ Break
11.00	▶ Do the ideas measure as one big group, working on the recently improved ideas from the previous round
11.45	▶ Split team into new groups, each taking away one of the ideas to improve using the improvements identified by the ideas measure tool ▶ Present back improved ideas to team
12.45	▶ Workshop leader talks about next steps and actions ▶ Closing comments
13.00	▶ Workshop ends

Ask yourself

▶ How can we build on the work that has already been done on these ideas?

▶ What kind of people will be good to have in this workshop?

▶ How can you keep the tone constructive and positive?

▶ What are the main criteria we will use to evaluate these ideas in future?

▶ Who will we present the improved ideas to, and what do they expect?

16

Creating new directions

'Companies fail to create the future not because they fail to predict it, but because they fail to imagine it.'

Gary Hamel

Use for: creating new ideas that make a team go in a new direction

When an organisation has tried to do something for a long time and realises it needs to change direction, the people in the team can feel pessimistic about the lack of success so far, or concerned about what the future might hold. Both attitudes will stand in the way of a successful workshop, because new directions are hard to imagine at first. The best way to help people see new possibilities is to change the way they feel about the topic.

The workshop objective: to help people overcome the fear of change and create new ideas they believe in

Great ideas come from a well-developed creative intuition, a gut reaction to what you see happening around you translated into an improvement or innovation.

Creative intuition suffers from ageing just like our bodies do. As we get older, live more stressed lives, work harder at more complicated jobs, our intuition suffers because we are not as stimulated by the outside world any more. We need something powerful to help us understand why a change of direction is necessary.

The power of personal experience

To keep the team's creative intuition strong, the workshop leader must find ways to help teams consider what is happening in the world outside of their immediate work. It's not enough to hear about changing trends from a debrief – people need to understand the changes personally. A visceral experience develops an emotional understanding, which leads to new ideas. If you are leading a workshop to help people create new directions, don't just ask people to think about that topic or read about it; ask them to do something themselves that proves why they need to take a new approach. That way they own the experience, and they bring their personal passion and opinions to the session. When people arrive at the workshop they are ready to discuss their experiences and use them to inspire new ideas.

Personal experience examples

Here are some personal experience tasks from past workshops I've led:

▶ On a project about buying health products, we asked the team to each go to a pharmacy and buy an embarrassing product in public, asking the pharmacist for advice on how to use it, in front of other people. This made people understand how their customers might feel when they were shopping for products related to ageing or ill health, and inspired ideas for how to make finding information and advice easier and less public.

▶ On a project about more convenient laundry products, we asked the team to do something really inconvenient for a week before the workshop (such as never take a lift, boil water in a pot on the stove, stop using their mobile phone). This was for a team who wanted to understand the life of an average mum with kids, how much laundry she needed to do and all the minor inconveniences she faced. Making them experience minor inconveniences regularly led to them understanding the benefits of convenience and how it was experienced, which they then used to create new, more convenient product ideas.

▶ On a project about digital behaviours among older people, we asked the team to sign up to and use a social media platform they had not tried before. When people went beyond Facebook and tried Instagram, Twitter and even Tinder, they developed a sense of how older people might be concerned about sharing their personal details online, which helped them think of ways to reassure their older target audience about buying products online.

Beyond changing how people feel, there are some workshop tools that help people to change their views and create new directions.

Rule breaker tool

The rule breaker is a simple and effective way to help people think controversially about the topic at hand and come up with rule breaking ideas.

1 Consider the topic of the workshop and list 10 or more rules that are typically followed. So, for example, if you are thinking about customer service, the rules are that the customer comes first, the staff are friendly, the phones are answered quickly, etc.

2 Then take the list of rules and write down the exact opposites, making these as extreme as possible. At this point remind your team that these are not ideas – these are simply new angles to think from. So with our customer service example, here are some broken rules:

 ▶ The customer comes first – the company comes first.

 ▶ The staff are friendly – the staff are rude.

 ▶ The phones are answered quickly – we stop answering our phones.

3 Finally, use the broken rules as angles for fresh thinking about new directions. For example:

 ▶ The company comes first – may lead to ideas about prioritising the most important customers who spend the most with the company.

 ▶ The staff are rude – may lead to ideas about the staff having their own complaints line to call for advice on how to deal with truly difficult customers and seek support.

 ▶ We stop answering our phones – may lead to an idea that we encourage customers to email their customer service requests to us with a brief description, so that the team can phone them back having prepared a response or solution.

Steps 1 and 2 can be done as a large team, with people calling out their answers, or in smaller teams. For this, though, it is important that the workshop leader shows an example of a couple of the rules being broken, or you will find people play the broken rules too safe, or that they misunderstand the exercise and try to create ideas immediately.

Step 3 should be done in small groups by giving each group one of the broken rules as a new angle to create many new ideas around, or using the entire list as inspiration for ideas.

Rule breaker Deodorant

	A		B
	Write the rules of the product or category (Do this side first)		Then write here the complete opposite of this rule, making these extreme opposites
01	Wear every day	01	Wear it once a year, only at Christmas
02	Smells nice	02	Makes you smell disgusting
03	Protects against body odour	03	Encourages your body to produce more odours
04	Long-lasting protection	04	Only lasts 30 seconds before you have to reapply
05	Invisible	05	Leaves a strong blue dye on your skin
06		06	
07		07	
08		08	
09		09	
10		10	

Rule breaker

Myths and truths tool

A good way to help people change their viewpoint and get inspired for new ideas is by using a myth-buster approach. This is particularly effective when a team have some misconceptions that are getting in the way of new directions or ideas. For example, a team could misunderstand how people use their product, be unclear on what customers really need or imagine customer stereotypes that are in fact wrong.

The reason this works well is that the team are taken on a journey of understanding. As a workshop leader you first show you understand what they believe the truth to be; next, you show how that truth is in fact a myth that needs to be changed; and finally you reveal the new truth, which becomes a fresh angle that people can use to inspire ideas for new directions.

Unlike the rule breaker (that the team produce together and in the moment), this tool is prepared in advance by the workshop leader. It can cause controversy and debate, depending on how tough you are about your myths and truths. As long as you plan well, this debate can be very energising for creating ideas.

How to use myths and truths

1 Before the workshop, decide which myths you want to bust, selecting between 3 and 10 depending on the nature of the topic. Make sure these myths are commonly held opinions among the team and recognisable so that the team hardly question them. For example:

▶ Myth 1 – We know people aren't using our products in the right way.

▶ Myth 2 – Our customers know we always provide quality.

▶ Myth 3 – We are sure that people trust our company.

2 Consider ways of busting those myths with evidence you have. Think about attention-grabbing, more controversial statements that can surprise or even shock the team. Work on what the main change or truth message is – it could be that the myth is actually correct but not taken seriously enough, or it could be totally wrong and the reverse is true. For example:

▶ Myth 1 – We know people aren't using our products in the right way. Truth: people believe their way is the right way, and so we will never change how they use our products.

▶ Myth 2 – Our customers know we always provide quality. Truth: quality is a given; people need more than quality as a reason to choose our products.

▶ Myth 3 – We are sure people trust our company. Truth: our older customers trust us, but the new customers we want to attract have no idea who we are.

3 Use the truths as new angles to start creating new ideas. For example:

▶ Truth: people believe their way is the right way – this could lead to ideas about how to change our products to better fit how people use them, rather than trying to change how people use the product.

▶ Truth: quality is a given; people need more than quality as a reason to choose our products – this could lead to ideas that build on quality, but also provide new, unique benefits versus competitors.

▶ Truth: our older customers trust us, but the new customers we want to attract have no idea who we are – this could lead to a new strategy for raising awareness among potential customers.

A fun way to run this tool is to make it into a pub quiz or game show-style competition. Split the team into small groups, or have people work individually on the answers. Set up the myths as questions with the potential answers as the truths that the team can guess or choose from. Have the team commit to their answers before you reveal the correct ones, and give points for correct answers.

Turning this tool into a game makes it enjoyable and competitive, which can be energising for the team, so long as the topic is appropriate. Beyond that, I find that if people have to guess the answer first, they listen far more closely to the truth, rather than just hearing it as a presentation. Be sure to end with the team committing to what they will do differently as a result.

Tips for turning an exercise into a game

▶ Make it fun, put on a quiz show host persona, get people involved, give it a funny name.

▶ Create cards, quiz sheets and other stimuli to help people get involved.

▶ Use films, music and prizes to add excitement, making sure that you focus on bringing to life the truths more than the myths.

▶ Be careful not to get too carried away – even though the game is fun, it should not take time away from using the outputs of the game for new ideas.

Creating new directions workshop plan (4-hour workshop)

Time	Task
09.00	▶ Welcome + objective + reminder of creative behaviours
09.10	▶ Participants introduce themselves by talking through a personal experience they have thought about in advance of the workshop ▶ They each write three separate Post-its on how the experience felt and what they learned, and hand these to the workshop leader

96

Time	Task
09.30	▶ Workshop leader themes the Post-its into groups and splits the team into groups of three ▶ Each group is given one theme from prep task 1 and they use the Post-its within that theme as new angles to give them three new direction ideas ▶ Each group presents their ideas back
10.00	▶ Workshop leader splits team into pairs, making sure everyone works with someone new ▶ Ask each pair to do a rule breaker activity, writing out the rules of the topic and then breaking those rules in extreme and controversial ways ▶ Each pair uses the broken rules as new angles to create three new direction ideas ▶ Each group presents their ideas back
11.00	▶ Break
11.15	▶ Workshop leader splits team into new groups of three, making sure everyone works with someone new for this last round ▶ Present the myths and truths as a game show, giving prizes to the team who have the most correct answers ▶ Each group uses the new truths as inspiration to create three new direction ideas inspired by prep task 3 ▶ Each group presents their ideas back
12.15	▶ Workshop leader reminds the team of the workshop objective and criteria for choosing next steps ▶ Team vote on their favourite ideas/idea themes to develop further
12.30	▶ Workshop leader splits the team into new groups of three, with each group taking one of the best ideas or themes to develop into actions and next steps ▶ Closing comments from each team member
13.00	▶ Workshop ends

Ask yourself

▶ What can you do to enable people to have a new experience?

▶ How can you encourage them to break an idea down into parts so it is easier to work on?

▶ How can you make people feel differently about the topic?

▶ How can you bring the outside world into the session?

17

Creating a new story about something old

Use for: changing the story people will tell others

Why would you want to tell a new story about something old? Organisations sometimes have a product, technology or message that has become exhausted and old. People can become so familiar with a message that they become blind to it (for example, health and safety signs that people stop reading after a time). It could be a story that is untrue and needs to be corrected (such as an incorrect rumour that keeps circulating), or something that happened in the past which you would like people to move on from (such as a negative news story that people still remember years later).

The workshop objective: to refresh the way your customers or team see you, your brand, your organisation or the promises you make about your products

Telling a story is our way of sharing memories, lessons learned and our values. Stories carry memorable meaning and information. Stories are psychologically powerful. If you work in sales or marketing, you will know that stories are more powerful than data when it comes to persuasion.[1]

Stories become self-fulfilling. The story that people tell about a topic, product or organisation can make it succeed or fail. It is therefore very important for a team to create a story that they feel is authentic and true for them, is positive and inspirational, and is something that they want to hear repeated back to them by customers. The act of retelling an old story in a new way redefines the language, tone and purpose of the subject.

Fairy tale tool

The fairy tale tool involves the team retelling an old story as a fairy tale, embellishing it and characterising it so that the elements of the story have more meaning. Retelling a story as a fairy tale is an excellent way to access meaning and uncover emotions, and works to expose elements and angles that otherwise you would have ignored. This leads to new ideas and angles, and the language used can inspire a better way of telling that story.

How to use the fairy tale tool

1 Ask the workshop participants to call out key elements of a fairy tale and write them down as they say them. For example:

   ▶ a hero

   ▶ a villain

   ▶ a journey

   ▶ a struggle

   ▶ a happy ending

   ▶ starts with 'once upon a time'

   ▶ has a moral or lesson.

2 Ask the workshop team to call out the best types of stories and write these in a list too. For example:

   ▶ a surprise ending

   ▶ unrequited love

   ▶ a bad person getting what they deserve

   ▶ you don't know what you've got until it's gone.

3 Split the workshop into small teams. Ask each group to think about the workshop topic and make up a fairy tale about the topic that contains some of the elements just identified. Ask them to make up characters, consider who the hero is, what their journey is, who the villain is, what the moral of the story is and how the journey ends. For example:

   ▶ If the topic of the workshop is to tell a new story about an old brand that has updated itself, the fairy tale might be about an old knight who has almost reached the end of his life, who meets a witch who gives him a magic potion that makes him young again and ready to live a whole new life, renewed and strong once more.

4 Ask the teams to narrate their stories out loud in the manner of a fairy tale, while other team members take notes on the language, story and characters.

5 The teams then go back into their smaller groups and use the stories they created and the notes they took from the other stories as fresh angles for new stories ideas. For example:

   ▶ The magic potion that renews the knight might lead to a story of how skincare Brand X has reinvented itself by taking in something 'magic', for example a new team of people, a new set of values or a new strategic direction for the future.

An insurance story

I once used the fairy tale tool with an insurance company, asking the people there to tell us a story about how insurance works. One of the most surprising stories that came back was that of a dark overlord living in a tall white ivory tower. The people who lived in the muddy lands below the tower were paying rent to him, but he didn't ever help or save them.

This story was a completely new angle to look at the company from and it led to many ideas about how to reassure loyal customers that the company treated claims carefully and wanted to find ways of paying out rather than not. It led to ideas for quicker turnaround times on claims and people being offered help immediately even if their claim was still being assessed.

Newspaper tool

When you want to make sure that the story your team will tell is memorable, the newspaper tool is ideal. This identifies the main headline that can cut through and grab attention. It also helps to identify the main elements of the story that need more detail beyond the headline.

1 Prepare some newspaper templates in the style of the publication and buy some actual copies of the newspaper too. Make sure you get a good range so that there is a mixture of tone and type of reader across the selection.

2 Give each team a different newspaper template, so for example one gets *The Sun*, one the *Financial Times*, one *Private Eye*, along with the actual copies.

3 Ask each team to create a news headline in the style of that publication and add in the main story below. Also encourage them to produce a diagram or picture to bring the story to life.

4 Get teams to read out their headlines and stories, presenting their newspapers to each other.

5 Ask the teams to go back into their smaller groups to use the newspapers they created to inspire new ways of telling the brand's story.

For example:

The Daily Paper

Headline

Anti-ageing injection for Brand X

Main story

Skincare Brand X has given itself an anti-ageing boost by launching its first innovation apprenticeship programme. Marketing, R+D, HR, Sales and Insights in all major regional hubs will commit to taking in five fresh apprentices every year to contribute to innovation thinking across the company. Building on its strong heritage in traditional skincare, the company will explore new, contemporary innovations to meet the needs of younger consumers across the world.

In other related news

Shares in Brand X's main competitor dropped this week...

Newspaper tool

Storyboard tool

Another simple storytelling technique is the storyboard. Because it asks people to break down whatever message they are trying to get across into six parts, it makes sure that people consider the flow of information and what is heard when.

Once the team have an idea of the kind of story they would like to tell, ask them to imagine the story as a 30-second advert, or a 6-box cartoon, or a quick film trailer. When teams work through their story and plot it within a storyboard structure, it makes them much more conscious of the importance of order and flow in how they tell that story.

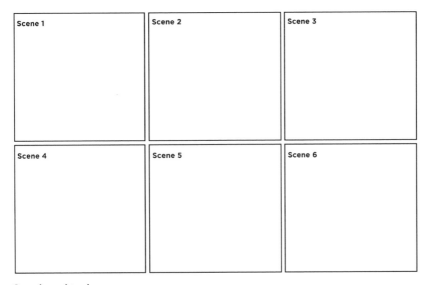

Storyboard tool

Creating new stories workshop plan (4-hour workshop)

Time	Task
09.00	▶ Welcome + objective + reminder of creative behaviours
09.10	▶ Participants introduce themselves by telling the team which fairy tale they like most and why ▶ They each write three separate Post-its explaining why they chose that fairy tale and hand these to the workshop leader

Time	Task
09.30	▶ Workshop leader themes the Post-its from the prep task into groups and splits the team into groups of three
	▶ Each group is given one theme from prep task 1 and they use the Post-its within that theme as new angles to give them three ideas for how to tell their story differently
	▶ Each group presents their ideas back
10.00	▶ Introduce the fairy tale technique, listing the elements of a good story first as a group, and some examples of what makes a story great
	▶ Split the team into new groups of four, making sure everyone works with someone new
	▶ Each team develops their fairy tale and presents it back as a story to the other team members who write notes as they listen
	▶ Fairy tale groups go back into their teams and use their stories and the notes they took as angles for three new ideas on how to tell the story differently
	▶ Teams present their ideas back
11.30	▶ Break
11.45	▶ Workshop leader splits team into new groups of three, making sure everyone works with someone new for this last round
	▶ Introduce the newspaper templates and ask teams to complete them
	▶ Teams present their newspapers back to the group who write notes while they listen
	▶ Teams go back into their newspaper groups and use their template and notes as inspiration to create three new ideas to tell the story in a new way
	▶ Each group presents their ideas back
12.30	▶ Workshop leader reminds the team of the workshop objective and criteria for choosing next steps
	▶ Team vote on their favourite stories to develop further
12.45	▶ Workshop leader agrees which team members will work on the top stories and bring them back to the team within the next few days (this is because it's hard to craft stories in big groups)
	▶ Closing comments from each team member
13.00	▶ Workshop ends

Ask yourself

▶ Who is this story for?

▶ How do you excite people about something they already know so well?

▶ How can you generate language through story telling?

▶ How can you get participants to convey emotion through a story?

▶ What tools can you use to bring insights to life?

18

How to create new names

Use for: generating a new name for something

Naming workshops are the hardest workshops of all because it is almost impossible to come up with a good name without thinking of hundreds of bad names first. It can get exhausting coming up with lists of names and you can feel as though you aren't making progress. People can feel defeated and pessimistic and when that happens it becomes hard to motivate them to keep going. For this reason you must build in a lot of energy, reward, inspiration, excitement and stimulus to keep people interested.

The workshop objective: to generate lots of potential ideas in order to find a good one

In naming sessions, you often know what's not right immediately, but good names are not apparent straight away. It's only when you review them later that you realise you've got a good one. It is vital to build in time to digest the ideas between rounds, contemplate and let the names settle in your head before making decisions on which ones to go forward with.

To give your naming workshop the best possible chance of success, start with a clear brief.

The brief	Example
What kind of names are you looking for (including examples)?	If you are looking for name ideas for a protein snack bar, make it clear that you want ideas that are uplifting, energetic, easy to understand, one or two syllables, that put a smile on your face. Words like Salsa, Fresh, Breathe, Ocean, Happy, Lift.
What sort of names do you definitely not want (including examples)?	Complicated, worthy, sophisticated, clever or technical names that sound made up. Words like Organic, Ethical, Boswelox, Evolve.
Will the name be heard or read or both, and where?	It will mostly be read on pack on the supermarket shelf among snack food products. It should be easy to say so that people can recommend it to each other.
What message should the name convey?	It needs to say that this snack is healthy, light and will give you a natural and sustained boost of energy at any time of day.
Who is the target person for this name?	A man or woman aged between 25 and 45 who is fitness conscious for health and mood reasons (not for weight loss) and wants to feel good about themselves. Eating well is a big part of their fitness regime.

Naming prep task

Once you have your brief, it is very important for naming to send out a prep task. Because the success of naming is often in a volume of ideas, and because you want those ideas to be as diverse as possible (so that the team come up with unique thoughts rather than influencing each other), asking each team member to create a list of names in advance of the workshop will save time on the day and allow you to theme and identify strong areas and weaker areas to plan for in the workshop design.

Send the naming brief to the team before the workshop and ask for at least 20 ideas for names from each person attending before the workshop. This encourages people to bring their individual meaning to the objective. It also stops people from trying to come up with the right answer first time.

As the workshop leader, you can theme these names and present the most popular themes at the beginning of the workshop, then use the themes as fresh angles for new name ideas.

Naming tools

Name generation needs even more tools options than other idea generation because you use up stimulus and inspiration very quickly and idea sessions go much faster. Here are some ideas for naming games.

Language packs

▶ Collect a range of language examples that relates in some way to the topic. For the protein snack bar names, collect pamphlets, website print-outs and any packaging examples from health food shops, perfumeries, pharmacies, cosmetics counters, gyms and doctors' surgeries. Buy newspapers and magazines about natural living, fitness and healthy eating. Go into second-hand bookstores and buy fiction and non-fiction books about gardening, food and health, or go online and print lots of different examples of language from a variety of websites.

▶ In the workshop, split the various types of language into themes and give different sets to small working teams, asking them to leaf through them for inspiration for name ideas.

Language mind map

▶ Using a mind map template, give different teams four names to kick off with. Ask them to do a mind map of word associations around each name, thinking spontaneously and writing quickly.

▶ It's important to explain that team members need not agree with each other, they are simply after many associations. For this reason, give a pen to everyone in the team rather than to just one person. At this point the associations do not need to be name ideas – they are just the new angles.

▶ Once they've done one round, choose some of the best word associations and do another layer of associations from those.

▶ Once the team have filled the page with word associations, each team can use the words on their template to generate new name ideas.

Language mind map

Dictionary games

▶ Provide a collection of dictionaries and thesauruses and ask the team to each choose one. Ask each person to randomly open their dictionary and point to a word. Ask them to choose a different page and point to another word. Ask them to individually combine those words into one. Then get team members to pair up and combine their words for some fresh angles to the new names.

Play the playlist

▶ Create a music playlist related to the topic, playing about 20 seconds of each song while people take notes of any good words or phrases they hear, or just doodle and draw as they listen. When the playlist is finished, get people into teams to use their notes to come up with new name ideas. Play the full playlist in the background while they do this.

Ideas cascade

▶ In silence, each person writes down five ideas for new names on a piece of paper, with a line drawn down the middle. After two minutes, each person passes the paper to their neighbour, who uses the ideas already written as new angles for new name ideas. The process is repeated until each person gets their original sheet back, with lots and lots of builds. If you have a big group, split teams into groups of five to do this task. Finally, get people to circle any words they think are good on the page and then use those circled to inspire some new name ideas.

Alphabet soup

▶ Split the team into groups of three and ask each group to come up with a new name for every letter in the alphabet, writing them as they go. Circle the best ones to build into new names.

Multi-sensory stimuli

▶ Even though naming is based on language, don't forget to use multi-sensory stimuli to help inspire ideas. A good way to do this is to prepare several boxes of relevant multi-sensory stimuli for teams to unpack, open, taste, touch, smell and try out. For the protein snack bar names, I would prepare boxes containing fitness accessories such as weights, a yoga mat, a headband or some sunglasses. Have some shampoo, skincare and deodorant products that are used by the target. Select some drinks, supplements, fruit and other snacks they might consume. Include DVDs they might have in their collection and even electronic items like a phone preloaded with health and wellbeing apps.

A story about ant scouts

'A single ant or bee isn't smart, but their colonies are.'

Peter Miller

Ant colonies send out scouts to find new nests when their nest is no longer safe. Scouts tend to be the older, more experienced ants. They each go out alone and in different directions to search for a new possible nest location on behalf of the colony. If they find somewhere good, they find another scout and by conferring and comparing whose area is better the scouts form a quorum of agreement that tells the colony where to move.[1] In this way they manage to find the best new nest because they initially go out alone and don't influence each other until they find something good.

▶

It is important for people attending a workshop to act like ant scouts and form their own opinions, collecting their own ideas in advance of the session, so that these diverse viewpoints can be shared. The risk in not doing this is that the team act like sheep, not ants, and simply follow each other, which means they do not explore a full range of ideas. This is why a prep task (in this case 20 new names before the workshop) is so valuable.

Other tips for naming

▶ Naming is tiring, so I'd recommend spending no more than three hours in a naming workshop.

▶ Set expectations on the number of names you want and number them as you go. Setting a high target helps people to feel encouraged to keep going and stops them from trying to create the right answer first time. I would say that you should create at least a couple of hundred ideas before looking back on them.

▶ Keep up the energy and pace by changing the number of people in each team, moving people around, getting them to stand, moving outside and making the exercises short. This energy will leave people feeling inspired and driven to keep going.

▶ Send out the full list of name ideas after the workshop and ask team members to give their feedback in a few days about which ones they really like – this is so that people get a chance to reflect on the ideas; often some new favourites emerge.

Creating new names workshop plan (3-hour workshop)

Time	Task
09.00	▶ Welcome + objective + reminder of creative behaviours
09.10	▶ Workshop leader presents the names sent in prior to the workshop and themes similar suggestions together ▶ Then asks each person to say their favourite name, which they created before the workshop, and why
09.30	▶ Split the team into groups of three ▶ Each group is given one of the name themes and they use the names grouped under that theme as new angles to produce 20 new name ideas ▶ Each group presents their ideas back

Time	Task
10.00	▶ Split the team into new groups of four, making sure everyone works with someone new ▶ Introduce language packs, asking each team to leaf through them in order to generate angles for 20 new name ideas ▶ Teams present their ideas back
10.30	▶ Break
10.45	▶ Introduce the playlist tool, asking each team to listen and write notes and ideas ▶ Ask the team to work in pairs, sharing their notes and generating angles for 20 new name ideas ▶ Teams present their ideas back
11.15	▶ Introduce the ideas cascade tool, asking people to write ideas and rotate them to the next person ▶ Ask the team to work in new pairs afterwards, sharing their notes and generating angles for 20 new name ideas ▶ Teams present their ideas back
11.45	▶ The team read all the names generated so far, each choosing their top five ideas ▶ The workshop leader advises the team that they will get a full list of the ideas written up to consider and reflect on ▶ Closing comments from each team member
12.00	▶ Workshop ends

Ask yourself

▶ What proportion of the time will we spend generating, and then reviewing?

▶ What tool will we use to create names?

▶ How will you encourage people to use different language?

▶ How will you keep up energy levels?

19

Customer needs workshops

Use for: improving the way we meet customers' needs

When you are leading a workshop to help a team better meet their customers' needs, the first step is to make sure everyone in the team has recently talked to their customer, consumer or end user about the workshop topic. For a charity this would be the charity beneficiaries or donors; for a management group this would be its staff; for brands this is the consumers of the brand. Hearing customers talk is vital, because how they express their needs is a rich form of inspiration. When team members repeat the language of the customers they talked with, they build a strong shared understanding of what customers need across the team, identifying themes that lead to new ideas.

The workshop objective: identifying customer needs to build better ways to meet them

Whether you have lots of market research or none at all, everyone coming to the workshop should have had a recent conversation with their target person on the topic of the workshop objective. It's not enough to have read a research report on the subject; they need to have heard it face to face and in the customer's own language.

If there is already a wealth of research, the conversation with the customer will bring to life those insights for you in a rich and meaningful way. If there is no research available to review, then it is all the more important to talk to customers beforehand.

How to talk to customers

As a workshop leader, you may find it difficult to persuade the team to talk to their customers. People are under time pressure and this might be seen as extra work. You will need to explain why this is necessary and how to go about it. Make sure people understand this is an interesting task that will prepare them for the workshop and may simply be a 15-minute conversation, so it should not feel onerous or challenging. Consider:

▶ having customers in the workshop with you

▶ finding customers to talk to in advance through friends and family networks

▶ talking via phone or video calls if customers are in different places

▶ using a professional recruitment company if your customers are hard to find.

What to talk to customers about

Use no more than five carefully worded, open-ended questions covering the following points:

1 Who are they? (Ask them about themselves, their family, their work and their general life.)

2 How does our organisation/brand/product feature in their life? (Ask how aware they are, when they use it, how important it is to them.)

3 What are the most positive aspects of being our customer? (What do we do that's better than the competition, what are the best aspects of the products you buy, what do we do well as a management team for you?)

4 What improvements could be made? (How can we improve our service to you, how could we make our product better, how could we do a better job for our customers?)

5 What advice would you give us to improve the way we serve customers like you? (How can we improve our offer in the next five years, is there anything we are not doing that we could start doing, do you have any other feedback?)

Make sure that the team are clear that they should write down the customers' answers to the questions word for word. This is because the words and phrases people use in informal conversation offer rich inspiration.

A story in three words

A workshop I once ran aimed to create ideas to help older people to feel more confident buying products online. We had many pieces of research to review and the team each visited the homes of several older people who were comfortable going online and several who were not. One of the most resonant quotes we heard was from a woman who wanted to do more online but was worried that she would 'break the internet'. In those three words we were able to understand just how concerned some people could be about doing the wrong thing online.

Theming customer needs

It is crucial to turn the customer interviews into some clearly defined need areas, so that you can deal with each need area in turn when generating ideas.

When the interviews are completed, theme the answers in preparation for the workshop. Print out all the notes from the interviews and cut out each sentence or section, grouping them according to theme. The themes should be based around the customers' needs, not the interview questions.

For example, you might find that one customer mentions the convenience of the packaging in the question about the advantages of this product over a competitor's product, and another customer mentions that they want the packaging to be even more convenient in the question about what we could do to improve our product. Even though the answers are from two different questions, they will both fit within a theme of 'making packaging as convenient as possible'.

Stick all the answers for each theme on one flipchart sheet, so that you have several different posters to put up in the workshop for people to read. Put the name of the theme on each poster and decorate the posters with images and magazine cut-outs that bring each theme to life.

If you have a wealth of research about your customers as well as these interviews, make sure that the posters also include key evidence, statistics or conclusions from past research. I tend to print out the most important conclusion slides from any past work and add them to the posters.

Why create posters?

▶ Posters are visually powerful, and having them in hard copy in the room rather than summarised onto PowerPoint slides means that they can be visible from the start, and throughout, for people to be inspired by.

▶ Instead of summarising the interview themes in my own words, I deliberately keep the actual words and phrases that the team sent in, so that all the different language can be read on each poster. This keeps the rich first-hand tone of the customers' voices, and it also helps the team to feel included because they can read their own interview quotes and see how they relate to the overall themes.

▶ Sometimes people send in handwritten notes, or use different fonts, levels of detail and even photos. These all provide visual richness and variety, which means the posters themselves are interesting to read and you may discover nuggets that lead to ideas.

▶ Posters are a much more powerful way of helping bring to life customer needs and make them memorable for the team beyond the workshop (you can even have them laminated and keep them as a reminder during future work).

Finding the meaning within the themes

Research has shown that people will be far more committed to a conclusion if they feel they discovered it themselves rather than hearing it from someone else.[1] After forming and naming the themes, a great way to get the team owning and believing in the customer needs is to hand over the interpretation of those themes to the team.

How to create meaning in teams

▶ Split the team into small groups and ask each to work on one or two of the themes. You can either ask each team to choose which themes they'd like to work on, or assign them yourself, having carefully considered who will work together best on which theme. For example, I sometimes ask the most pessimistic person on the team to join the group that is working on a theme full of product benefits or advantages. Likewise, I select the most positive person to join the group who will discuss a challenging theme or area of weakness.

▶ Send each group away to read all the different quotes within that theme, and ask them to come back having summarised the main needs and opportunities that come from it.

▶ To make sure teams come back with comparable work, give them a template or structure to follow, for example come back with the top three insights and the top three opportunities this theme inspires.

▶ Teams present these back to each other and so the analysis and implications have been shared across the teams. In debating and discussing them they have even greater familiarity with the customer themselves.

Workshop to better meet customers' needs (4-hour workshop)

Time	Task
09.00	▶ Welcome + objective + reminder of creative behaviours
09.10	▶ Participants introduce themselves and briefly mention who they interviewed as a prep task and any immediate insights they got from that interview
09.30	▶ Workshop leader presents the themed posters that outline the main needs emerging from the interviews ▶ Split the team into groups of three and ask them each to choose one or two posters to work on (depending on how many posters there are and how many teams you have) ▶ Each group is given an instruction and template to analyse the posters to identify the top three insights and the top three opportunities within that theme ▶ Each group presents their ideas back and sticks the insights and opportunities templates on the wall next to the relevant poster
10.30	▶ Break
10.45	▶ Workshop leader splits team into new groups of three, making sure everyone works with someone new ▶ Ask each group to choose one theme (poster and insights + opportunities template) ▶ Each group uses the poster and template to create 10 new ideas for how to meet that particular need ▶ Each group presents their ideas back
11.00	▶ Workshop leader splits team into new groups of three, making sure everyone works with someone new for this last round ▶ Give each group an idea stretcher template and ask them to write down their top four ideas from the last round in the left-hand column. Then fill in the completely mad and finally innovative and ambitious versions of that idea ▶ Each group uses the completed template as inspiration to create three new ideas (or improvements on existing ideas) for meeting customers' needs ▶ Each group presents their ideas back

▶

117

Time	Task
11.45	▶ Workshop leader reminds the team of the workshop objective and criteria for choosing next steps ▶ Team vote on their favourite ideas for meeting customers' needs better, to develop further
12.00	▶ Workshop leader splits the team into new groups of three, with each group taking one of the best ideas to develop into actions and next steps ▶ Teams present back their developed ideas and action plans ▶ Closing comments from each team member
13.00	▶ Workshop ends

Ask yourself

▶ How will we help everyone to talk to their customer?

▶ What insight would we like the participants to gain from speaking to their customers?

▶ How will we identify the main customer needs?

▶ How will we create ideas from the most important needs?

20

CHAPTER TWENTY
Roadmaps

Use for: understanding why and how to create a five-year roadmap

A roadmap is a detailed plan that helps the team anticipate the future, usually within a defined time period of at least five years. The roadmap shows a set of ideas and how those ideas build from the present towards the future. It helps to define how to get from now to the future, and to time initiatives and actions to make sure you have started early enough to make ideas happen at the right time.

The workshop objective: to create a set of ideas that stretches into the longer term

There are various reasons why you might choose to lead a roadmap workshop, for example:

▶ to create an ambitious mid- to long-term plan to maximise an opportunity for business, market, technology or consumer change

▶ to look five years into the future to establish a far more ambitious short- and medium-term plan

▶ to release a team from worrying about the here and now by inspiring them with trends and opportunities, and allowing them to optimistically construct the future.

Roadmap projects

Examples of roadmap projects I've worked on are:

▶ **The future of laundry:** consider demographic, economic and environmental trends (such as water shortage) in order to develop laundry ideas for 10 years' time. The roadmap will plan which technologies research and development will begin working on and when.

▶ **Breakthrough mobile phone devices:** consider mobile phone user behaviours and technology trends to begin to plan for the next generation of mobile phones that will be on the market in five years' time.

▶ **Sustainability:** consider how attitudes to sustainable products differ between consumers in developed versus developing markets, and plan how to convert each market to more sustainable products over the next five years (with each market moving at a different pace).

Why create a five-year roadmap?

'We tend to overestimate the effect of a technology in the short run and underestimate the effect in the long run.'

Roy Amara

Whether looking at new consumer needs, emergent technology, societal trends or market shifts, we tend to overestimate the short-term change or opportunity (because it doesn't happen quickly enough or is not immediately successful) and therefore we forget to plan for opportunity in the medium and long term. A five-year plan helps to identify how different projects might have an impact on each other, or benefit each other over time, instead of focusing on one initiative only.

The internet will never catch on...

I remember a senior media executive once interrupting a trends talk I was giving to say, 'Sorry, but may I just check, has anyone here ever actually uploaded or downloaded anything from the internet?' When she looked around the room, the other senior executives were shaking their heads, dismissing 'the internet' as a passing fad.

Big trends are easier to ignore than to face, especially if you're not sure how to approach them. The roadmap provides a safe structure to make sure teams face trends and work logically on how to anticipate them in enough time to make them an opportunity rather than a risk to the organisation.

Future trends prep task

Prep tasks are important when it comes to future trends. While it's often useful to bring in a future trends expert to speak, there is the risk that participants will feel sceptical of the trends identified – and therefore not feeling aligned with them. I find it more useful to ask the participants to offer their own opinions of the important future trends as a key input to the workshop. You can also invite future trends experts to speak, but encouraging the team towards a future-facing mind set adds to this expertise and prepares them to contribute, listen and debate.

1 A few weeks before the workshop send an invitation asking each participant to think of a market, consumer or technology trend that they know will affect the business in the next few years.

2 Provide a template for team members to fill in before the workshop, such as:

Title and brief description of the trend	Opportunities this trend offers us as a business:	Risks if we ignore this trend:
	1	1
	2	2
	3	3

3 Ask team members to send their completed templates to you a couple of days before the workshop.

4 Print each prep task and theme them into groups on another wall in the workshop, putting similar or related trends together and giving each group a title.

5 If you have a formal trends presentation or expert in your workshop, be sure to include their trends in your themes too.

6 Print some extra blank prep task sheets and give one to anyone who has not done their prep task as they walk in to complete before the session starts.

Roadmap tool

▶ In your workshop, create a big wall matrix that lays out the time scale on the horizontal axis, and different opportunity areas, technologies or customer on the vertical axis, for example:

	Year 1	Year 2	Year 3	Year 4	Year 5
Customer type A					
Customer type B					
Customer type C					
Other					

▶ As ideas are created through the day, ask the team to put them up on the wall matrix where they fit best.

▶ Through the day you will begin to see where you have a lot of ideas and where you need to create more, and this can help to direct your focus during the session.

▶ This matrix can also be used to stretch the very close ideas (years 1 + 2) and inspire new ideas for years 4 + 5, or take ideas from years 4 + 5 and bring them back to more feasible or earlier versions in years 1 + 2.

A roadmap workshop plan (6-hour workshop)

Time	Task
09.00	▶ Welcome + objective + reminder of creative behaviours
09.10	▶ Ask participants to introduce themselves and tell us the trend they identified for their prep task as an introductions exercise
09.30	▶ Formal presentation by future trends expert, R&D about new technologies, or research about changing customer attitudes, or anything to remind us what opportunities and challenges our business or organisation will face in future ▶ Team members take notes on ideas for the roadmap as they listen ▶ Q&A for understanding
10.30	▶ Workshop leader introduces the trends themes from the prep task (which also include the formally presented themes) ▶ Split the team into groups of three and ask each team to choose one or two trend themes posters to work on (depending on how many themes you have and groups to work on them) ▶ Ask each group to identify the top five opportunities or risks for their chosen theme ▶ Using those opportunities and risks, create at least three new ideas that are inspired by the previous task, one for years 1 + 2, the next for years 3 + 4 and the last for years 4 + 5 or beyond ▶ Teams present these ideas by reading them out and sticking them on the roadmap matrix in the relevant place

Time	Task
11.30	▶ Break
11.45	▶ Workshop leader splits team into new groups of three, making sure everyone works with someone new
	▶ Ask each group to choose one idea that they love from the matrix so far. If they've chosen a year 1/2 idea, ask them to stretch that idea to the future, adding at least one new idea per year taking that idea forward
	▶ If they've chosen a year 5 idea, ask that team to create a new idea for years 4, 3, 2 and 1 that makes that idea feasible and will build towards making the idea a reality
	▶ Finally, if they've chosen an idea in the middle of the time period, they need to create ideas for years 1 + 2 and years 4 + 5
	▶ Teams present back their new ideas and plot them on the wall matrix
12.45	▶ Workshop leader reminds the team of the workshop objective and criteria for choosing next steps
	▶ Team members each write down their favourite idea from the roadmap so far, one that has ideas from years 1–5, to develop further and hand this in to the workshop leader
13.00	▶ Lunch
	▶ Workshop leader themes main ideas and works out final working team members for each idea
13.45	▶ Workshop leader splits the team into new groups for each of the winning ideas
	▶ Each group takes one idea to develop into actions and next steps
	▶ Teams present back their developed ideas and action plans
14.45	▶ Discuss next steps and closing comments from each team member
15.00	▶ End

Ask yourself

▶ Why do we need to create a five-year roadmap?

▶ How will we transform opportunities into actions?

▶ Have you placed emphasis on the long-term results?

▶ How can you plan to stay ahead using a roadmap?

CHAPTER TWENTY-ONE

Alignment

> **Use for:** encouraging people to work towards an agreed goal
>
> Workshops are brilliant for aligning people. Alignment is crucial for any project so that people agree to follow the same expectations and work on something together.

The workshop objective: to get the team to agree and move on with actions

Your team don't need to completely disagree with each other to need alignment. Some examples of reasons for running an alignment workshop are:

▶ the team have different views on the importance of the project

▶ the team have different opinions about what direction the project should take

▶ the team have many different theories about what has happened so far that are stopping them from moving forward together

▶ the desired outcome of any alignment workshop is for people to 'draw a line in the sand' and agree to move forward together.

'Successful diplomacy is an alignment of objectives and means.'

Dennis Ross

Five steps to alignment

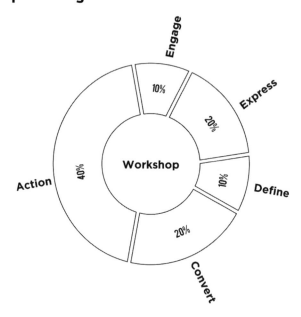

Pie chart of alignment

1 Engage people in the topic

This means immersing them in the topic in a rich and first-hand way. If people are bored by a topic, or feel distant from it, they might not give it much attention and so their decisions will be uninformed. When team members engage with a topic on a personal level, it creates a shared responsibility for the project and makes people feel more committed to it.

2 Express opinions and concerns

People are often unable to move on unless they feel they have truly been heard. If they think that a decision has already been made or is a foregone conclusion, they are less likely to align. It is important to allow time for team members to express their concerns or differing opinions in a structured manner, for example:

▶ ask for comments, points of view or disagreements to be collected in advance of the workshop

▶ structure the way they express themselves – for instance, ask each person to identify three opportunities for the project and three concerns. Collect these and theme them into groups for the team to work on in the next stage.

Preparing for alignment

I led a workshop for a sports brand to align the team members from five countries to produce one creative brief for their advertising. An ideal advert would reflect the local culture, clothing styles, people and even weather of each of the markets, so alignment was going to be difficult. We did a thorough analysis before the workshop, talking with all the different countries, reviewing their needs and ideas, and suggesting common ground. A presentation of this analysis started the workshop, and together we defined what was unacceptable for each market, what was acceptable but not ideal and what was ideal. Because each market felt their opinions had been fully expressed, we were able to align on the brief.

3 Define the issues

Once all the concerns are out in the open, use the time to define the important points to keep in mind when moving forward on the project. Put people into small working groups to define the key issues and keep moving them around so that they don't become attached to one issue.

For example, if one significant area of concern relates to the project being a waste of money, and another relates to the project not having enough time:

1 Split the team into two groups, putting the people who are most concerned with money in the money group.
2 Ask the money group to define what might cause money to be wasted.
3 Ask the time group to define the problems that might lead to time issues.

This gives each issue more dimension, which leads to a better perspective to work with later.

The money group might come back with these elements of how the project could waste money:

▶ It's not our area of expertise, so we will need to hire consultants.
▶ It's not well defined, so we have no idea how much it could actually cost.

▶ There's no proof it's going to work, so we might spend money on it for no results.

4 Convert the issues to opportunities

It is difficult to create ways forward if you have only challenges and concerns in mind. After defining the key concerns, ask your teams to turn those concerns into opportunities, ideas or questions, rephrasing each issue into a possibility and changing the way it is expressed into positive language, even if it is not a decision or idea yet.

For example, the team converting the money concerns might create the following opportunities:

Issue	Converted to an opportunity
It's not our area of expertise, so we will need to hire consultants.	This is the perfect chance for us to create this skill within our team.
It's not well defined, so we have no idea how much it could actually cost.	Let's write a clear brief together to make sure we understand the possible cost.
There's no proof it's going to work, so we might spend money on it for no results.	Could we run a pilot in one of our smaller stores to see what happens?

5 Agree next steps

At this point in the session your team should be able to agree on some next steps and actions, and be able to move forward in alignment.

Calibration tool

It is useful to run a calibration exercise to prevent people from making assumptions too early. The tool creates a list of dos and don'ts for the team to keep in mind in all the next stages.

How to use the calibration tool

▶ Prepare a series of subjects that the team need to agree on, for example:

  ▶ Who is our target consumer?

  ▶ What will we be able to make?

  ▶ What kind of impact will this have on our brand image?

Flipchart (cross and tick)

▶ Prepare a flipchart for each subject, dividing it into two columns. On the left-hand side of each flipchart, write what we are, and on the right what we are not. For example:

    ▶ Who is our target consumer? And who is not our consumer?

    ▶ What will we be able to make? And what will we not be able to make?

    ▶ What kind of impact will this have on our brand image? What kind of impact do we not want it to have?

▶ Ask each person in the team to consider each question individually and without discussion.

▶ Invite them to write as many statements as they can about each subject, each one on a separate Post-it, which they should then stick on the flipcharts.

▶ Once everyone has completed this, divide the team into separate groups, giving each group one flipchart to summarise. The groups each summarise the two sides of the flipchart by theming the Post-its and circling the themes with a title. For example:

▶ Who is our target consumer?

    – An everyday woman

    – Busy at home and at work

    – Wants to do a bit more exercise than she does

▶ And who is not our consumer?

    – A superwoman or perfectionist

    – Working in a high-pressure job

    – Obsessed with fitness and healthy diet

When these are summarised, you might find that some members of the team don't agree, or that two themes contradict each other. The team can then spend time debating those themes where people don't yet agree.

Alignment workshop plan (4-hour workshop)

Time	Task
09.00	▶ Welcome + objective + reminder of creative behaviours
09.10	▶ Engage: participants introduce themselves and briefly mention what they did as a prep task to engage in the topic before the workshop and any insights they got from that prep task
09.30	▶ Express: workshop leader presents the main issues and opinions that have already been expressed, inviting some discussion on each and being sure to hear from each person
10.30	▶ Break
10.45	▶ Define: workshop leader splits team into new groups of three, making sure everyone works with someone new ▶ Ask each group to choose one issue/opinion theme ▶ Each group uses the theme to define the main elements of that concern ▶ Each group presents their ideas back
11.15	▶ Convert: workshop leader splits team into new groups of three, making sure everyone works with someone new for this last round ▶ Ask each group to translate the issues and challenges into opportunities, ideas or questions ▶ Teams present back their ideas

Time	Task
11.45	▶ Agree: workshop leader asks the participants to individually work on each subject to be calibrated, writing down on Post-its underneath what the project will and won't be
	▶ Split the team into groups, each group taking one subject flipchart to theme the Post-its on both sides
	▶ Teams present back their calibration themes, inviting debate and discussion on any that are in conflict
12.30	▶ Agree: workshop leader reminds the team of the workshop objective and criteria for choosing next steps
	▶ Team vote on their favourite ideas, opportunities and questions from the previous two rounds
	▶ Team agree next steps and actions
	▶ Closing comments from each team member
13.00	▶ Workshop ends

Ask yourself

▶ How can we help the team to find common ground and work together?

▶ How can you divide the session between expressing concerns and moving forward?

▶ How can you make people feel comfortable expressing their concerns?

▶ How will the team be able to move forward after the session?

▶ How will we check that everyone leaves aligned?

CHAPTER TWENTY-TWO

Action planning

Use for: creating an action plan

A workshop can be a productive, creative and enjoyable day, but if nothing happens as a result of the session, the time will have been wasted.

The workshop objective: creating an action plan that people commit to delivering

There are three stages to action planning for a workshop:

1 Agree what we want to happen.

2 Agree who will take each action.

3 Follow up to check it is happening.

Agree what we want to happen

By the end of a workshop, if you've had time to vote on and prioritise ideas, and develop them a little, you probably have a good sense of the goal you are aiming for.

Identifying initiatives tool

If it's still unclear what the main initiatives are, a simple way to agree some end goals is to use an identifying initiatives tool, as follows:

1 Remind the team of the objectives of the workshop.

2 Ask the team to consider what specific initiatives or ideas they feel strongly should be taken forward.

3 Ask everyone in the team to read through all of the outputs and ideas from the whole session individually and without discussion, making some notes about possible initiatives or ideas.

4 When everyone is ready, ask them to write their initiatives separately, each on a big Post-it (A5) in full, descriptive sentences.

Name
A short memorable name for this initiative

Brief description

A couple of sentences describing why it's important and what it will achieve and by when

Other comments

Other ideas, thoughts or challenges to keep in mind

Identifying initiatives

5 When everyone has finished writing, ask them to share their initiatives, collecting them in themes as you go.

6 It will soon become clear where the team have similar ideas, and the visual nature of the themes means you will see how popular each idea is. You can then work on each in turn for action planning.

7 Once you've themed the initiatives, decide as a team which to focus on – you could do action planning around five, three or even just one.

This technique works well because:

▶ making people read everything from the workshop reminds them of ideas they may have forgotten

▶ asking people to read as individuals keeps their thinking truly diverse and so you are more likely to have a good spread of ideas

▶ creating a name for each initiative really helps to describe and sell the initiative internally

▶ asking people to write in full, descriptive sentences means you can combine the different sentences, which often leads to a far more inspiring description

▶ it is more thorough than simply voting on individual ideas – often the best ideas emerge as a combination of a few, or as a strong theme rather than single ideas.

Agree who will do what to make it happen

Make a commitment

'Setting a goal is not the main thing. It is deciding how you will go about achieving it and staying with that plan.'

Tom Landry

Research suggests that when we set a goal, we feel a sense of tension that we are driven to resolve and that lasts right up until we achieve that goal.[1] At the end of a workshop it is vital to set goals for how each person in the team will action or be a part of the outputs, so that your workshop has impact beyond the experience itself.

Accountability tool

Because the workshop leader has been in a position of authority when generating ideas, the people in the workshop may misunderstand your role and expect you to take all the actions afterwards. So at this point it is crucial to set up individual and group accountability for the next steps.

The accountability tool is a simple way of laying out how the initiatives will be achieved. Identify the initiatives and send small teams away to complete an accountability template, presenting it back to each other afterwards. Develop your own accountability templates, using language that your team will be familiar with.

Title	

Description of this project

Key elements	Opportunities

Challenges	Other details

Action to be taken in the next week to kick-start this initiative	Who will action

Action to be taken in the next month to kick-start this initiative	Who will action

Action to be taken by _____ / _____ / _____ (Insert date)	Who will action

Other	Names in group

Accountability template

Personal commitments

To make sure everyone remembers their personal contribution to the initiatives, end an action planning session by asking each team member to personally commit to something as a result of the workshop, for example:

▶ What do you commit to doing in the next week as a result of this workshop?

▶ What will you do differently as a result of this workshop?

▶ What will you do more of as a result of this workshop?

▶ What will you do less of as a result of this workshop?

Send a letter

Make the commitments powerful by asking people to write themselves a letter that will be sent to them at a later date.

▶ Give each person a piece of blank paper and an envelope (offer a variety of stationery to choose from, to make it more personal).

▶ Give them time to write themselves a letter that they will receive at a later date (a month, three months or even a full year later).

▶ In the letter they should remind themselves about what they are inspired to do and what they have committed to, or any advice they think might help them when they read their letter.

▶ It's important to point out that no one else will read the letters, so they can be as honest as they like.

▶ Once written, the team members seal the letters, write their address on the envelopes and give them to the workshop leader to post on the agreed date.

Follow up regularly on the action plan to see that it is being carried out

It is good practice to schedule both the workshop and a follow-up session a week or two later to keep up momentum for the outputs and actions.

Action planning workshop plan (4-hour workshop)

Time	Task
09.00	▶ Welcome + objective + reminder of creative behaviours
09.15	▶ As a team use the identifying initiatives tool ▶ This will decide on which initiatives to focus the action planning
10.15	▶ Split the team into small groups according to role or department ▶ Send them away to complete an accountability template ▶ Gather groups back together to present back
11.15	▶ Ask each individual to complete a personal commitment template inspired by their role in the templates just completed ▶ Share the commitments with the rest of the team
12.00	▶ Ask everyone to write themselves a letter, based on their accountability and commitments, personally reminding themselves about what they learned and how they felt in this session ▶ Explain that they are writing these to themselves only and will not be required to share what they write ▶ Hand out envelopes and ask people to seal their letters and put their name and address on the front. Collect these up and make a note of when they wish to have them posted back (e.g. six months' time)
12.30	▶ Gather the whole team together and schedule a follow-up session to check progress of actions ▶ Closing comments
13.00	▶ Workshop ends

Ask yourself

▶ Will the actions be completed without an action plan?

▶ How will you make sure people take accountability for the actions they have created?

▶ How will you make people commit to their goals?

▶ How will we know that the identified initiatives have been successful?

▶ When will you be able to follow these actions up?

23

CHAPTER
TWENTY-THREE

Defining purpose

Use for: defining a statement of purpose

More than ever we want to feel our work effort is not just for the money – we want our work to have meaning and somehow contribute to the lives of others. With time so pressured, people need to feel that their time is being used in a worthwhile manner – research has shown that people have a healthier outlook and feel less stressed when contributing towards a higher purpose.[1]

The workshop objective: to help a team find a higher purpose to their work that will motivate them to work better

A purpose can inspire your team to want to come to work in the morning, knowing they are having a positive impact on the lives of others. Purpose is often very aspirational – it might not be the case now, but it's what you aim to fulfil as an organisation in the near future. When a team create a purpose statement together, it can be far more powerful than simply being told what the company's purpose is.

'He who has a why to live for can bear almost any how.'

Friedrich Nietzsche

Unilever's purpose is to make a positive impact on the world through the brands it produces, including committing to managing environmental impact and making the business more sustainable. Kellogg's purpose is 'nourishing families so that they can flourish and thrive'.

The outcome of a purpose workshop is a purpose statement that motivates the team to work better, by recognising the contribution their work makes to the greater good.

Prep task ideas for purpose workshops

▶ **Inspiration from other organisations:** team members to get a sense of the phrasing and language that other companies use for purpose.

▶ **Good and bad examples:** team members to bring an example of one purpose statement they have found that they think is good and one that they think is awful, and be ready to describe the reasons behind both.

▶ **Talk to people close to the brand:** ask the team to talk to their staff, customers, competitors, shareholders or even critics about what they believe the company's purpose sould be, and bring those thoughts to the workshop.

Playfulness

When you are creating a sense of a positive future, it helps to use playfulness to access people's emotions. Taking people out of a work style that is very verbal or rational and letting them enjoy child-like play can stimulate deep inspiration for purpose.[2] Drawing, arts and crafts and sculpture can break the ice and release some of the emotions that make you feel a little bit more innocent and a little bit more positive, like a child.

Animal attraction

I was leading a workshop in an animal park because it was close to the client's office, and thought it might be good to ask to see some interesting animals at some point during the workshop as an energiser.

The workshop brought together a range of team members, each working in different departments for a big brand, and it soon became clear that they were all working at cross-purposes to each other on one of their most important target customer types. By mid-morning, the team were worried about achieving any kind of agreement.

After the morning break, as a surprise, the animal park staff brought in a hedgehog, a bearded dragon and a snake. The room erupted with excitement, and everyone forgot their roles and played together with the animals. When we started the next session people were noticeably more relaxed and positive, and were looking forward to working together on new solutions.

'Planet of...' tool

Starting with an idealistic or Utopian scenario helps the team tap into their hopes for how their work could benefit other people.

The 'planet of...' tool asks people to draw a visual expression of their ideals and aspirations. When they subsequently explain their drawings back to the group, it gives rich emotion and language that can inspire ideas for purpose.

How to use the 'planet of...' tool:

1 Split people into groups and give each group the 'planet of...' template along with a selection of coloured pens. Ask them to draw an impression of the perfect planet (related to the team's purpose).

   ▶ The perfect planet for a homeless charity might be the planet full of free bedrooms, duvets, pillows and heaters for any homeless people to use whenever they need to.

   ▶ The perfect planet for a shampoo brand might be a planet of beautiful, healthy, glossy-haired women who are happy and confident.

Planet of...

Perfect planet of bread

2 For example, the perfect planet of bread has a rich warm sun that's always at the right temperature. There is a family all around this beautiful piece of bread and bread is at the centre of the world. There is a river of natural

wholesome ingredients flowing into the bread and the smell coming from it fills the planet with deliciousness. This is a down-to-earth planet, familiar and inviting.

3 Encourage the team to have fun with their drawings and tell them not to be constrained by anything. Remember these planets, like all creative games, are simply a way of creating fresh angles to inspire new ideas – they are not the ideas themselves.

4 Once all the planets have been drawn, ask the teams to present them back to each other.

▶ For example, for a bread company you may hear phrases like 'the centre of the family', 'down to earth' and 'natural wholesomeness'.

▶ This language could lead to ideas for a purpose beyond just baking and selling bread, for example enriching people's lives by creating moments for extended families to come together and feel truly at home, or giving parents the confidence that they are giving their children the best possible nutrition every day.

5 When people are presenting, be as encouraging and positive as possible, and if appropriate applaud each team. While teams present, the teams listening should take notes about the language and descriptions used, as this is good language to inspire new ideas.

6 After the teams have presented, they should use their drawings and the notes they made as inspiration for ideas for several purpose statement ideas. As with every creative process, you will create a lot of possible purpose statements before finding one to agree on.

Instead of drawing a planet, you can do a similar exercise by asking the team to make up a bedtime story about the ideal world, or use magazine cut-outs to create a collage about the ideal world.

Sculpture competition tool

This is a great way to help people create ways of working, principles, values and emotions.

1 Prepare different packs of arts and crafts, building sets or children's play sets, with a different type of set for each group to use (e.g. one set of Play-Doh, one set of building blocks, one set of Lego, one box of arts and crafts materials, etc.).

2 Get the team into groups of three and lay out enough sets per team.

3 Tell them they have 20 minutes to make a sculpture that represents the best possible purpose that this team could achieve in future. After 20 minutes you will stop them and ask them to explain their sculpture, and there will be a prize for the best one.

4 When everyone is clear on the task, count them down (3, 2, 1, go!) to make it exciting and fun. You will find people really get into this with enthusiasm, and as well as being a great tool to use, it brings real energy to the day.

5 After 20 minutes, call time and ask the different teams to present their sculp-ture to each other and explain what it means and how it represents the purpose. Be sure to applaud each sculpture and team and keep up the energy.

6 After the teams have presented back, take a quick secret ballot vote (asking teams to write their favourite sculpture on a Post-its) and ask them to use their sculptures to create new purpose statements and language.

7 After the teams have presented these, award the prize to the team with the best sculpture.

Future headline tool

A more verbal exercise is the future headline tool, which helps team mem-bers to create an idealistic future, to inspire greater purpose.

1 Using a newspaper template, split teams into groups and ask them each to imagine an amazing future for the business in five years' time when the team will have made a real difference to people's lives through their work.

2 Teams fill out the newspaper template and present them back to each other, making notes on any ideas that occur to them.

3 Teams then use the newspaper headlines as inspiration for new ideas for their purpose statement. For example, in the bread project, a team might imagine a headline in a BBC *Good Food* magazine that reads 'Bread Changes Lives', going on to detail how the company managed to convert schools and sports clubs across the nation to eating wholemeal bread, and as a result they have discontinued their white bread ranges and can prove this reduced childhood obesity rates.

4 The newspaper headlines might lead to ideas for advertising campaigns, charity events, new products or innovative businesses.

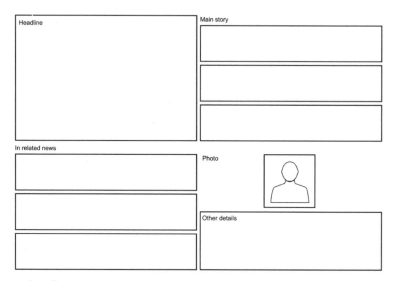

Future headline

Choosing the final purpose statement

When choosing between a lot of purpose statements to pick the best one, don't limit the team to choosing one existing statement. Rather, ask team members to work in pairs to read all the statements and language that have been created through the day, and to use their favourites to write their own purpose statement together.

Once these have been shared, work in a separate, smaller group after the workshop ends to use people's favourite ideas to refine your purpose. It is very difficult to craft the perfect purpose statement in a big group.

How to develop your final purpose statement

Ask:

▶ Is it inspiring, positive and rewarding to work in a company with this purpose?

▶ Is it simple enough to understand and remember the first time you hear it?

▶ Is it easy to explain to other people?

▶ Is it something you can use to guide any decisions you make in your work?

144

Purpose workshop plan (4-hour workshop)

Time	Task
09.00	▶ Welcome + objective + reminder of creative behaviours
09.10	▶ Participants introduce themselves and briefly describe their prep task 1 (bringing an example of one good purpose statement and one bad one), writing on separate Post-its the three reasons why they chose each one ▶ Workshop leader collects the purpose statements, putting all the good ones on one wall and the bad ones on another ▶ Collect the Post-its and theme them onto several flipcharts, giving each theme a name, such as 'uses everyday language' or 'sounds unrealistic'
09.30	▶ Split the team into groups of three and ask them each to pick one theme area to work with ▶ Each group uses their theme, as well as the good and bad purpose statements on the wall, as inspiration for at least three purpose statements for our objective ▶ Teams present back their purpose statements
10.15	▶ Break
10.30	▶ Workshop leader splits team into new groups of three, making sure everyone works with someone new ▶ Ask each group to share the results of prep task 2 (their interviews with customers, shareholders, etc.) with each other, and use these as a way of coming up with three more purpose statements per group ▶ Each group presents their ideas back
11.15	▶ Workshop leader splits team into new groups of three, making sure everyone works with someone new for this last round ▶ Give each team either a 'planet of...' template, sculpture competition or future headline tool, allowing them time to draw, build or complete it ▶ Teams present back their task and participants take notes of the language they use to describe their ideal scenario ▶ Each group then uses the completed tool as inspiration to create three new purpose statements ▶ Each group presents their ideas back
12.00	▶ Workshop leader reminds the team of the workshop objective and criteria for choosing a purpose statement ▶ Teams each read all the statements, language and stimuli from the workshop so far, and work in pairs to write one possible purpose statement together ▶ These are presented back and, if appropriate, the team vote on their favourite statements, words or language
12.45	▶ Workshop leader talks through next steps and actions to define the final purpose statement ▶ Closing comments from each team member
13.00	▶ Workshop ends

Ask yourself

▶ How can we get inspiration from other companies with purpose?

▶ How can we help people to be optimistic and aspirational?

▶ How can you incorporate play into the session?

▶ Who will develop the final purpose statement?

24

Working better together

Use for: changing the way a team works for the better

Every team gets to a point when they are working in an inefficient and/or outdated way and they need to improve.

The workshop objective: to help people create ideas that change the way they work for the better

This type of workshop takes the participants on a journey to recognise the change that's needed, create some possible ways of making that change, agree what the best ideas are, then work on putting these into action.

Self-generated discovery

Research has shown that the more in control we feel about a search for information, the more likely we are to believe in the results.[1] People are more emotionally committed to an answer that they themselves have researched and created.

There are five steps to a working better workshop:

1 Recognise the areas that need improvement.

2 Define those areas in a way that makes them very clear.

3 Generate lots of ideas for how those areas can be improved.

4 Choose the best ideas.

5 Work out an action plan to implement them.

Prep tasks for working better

A relevant prep task is vital to make sure the team are working with relevant information, otherwise you may arrive at the workshop to a team with a firm belief that everything is working just fine as it is or without having considered the topic deeply enough.

Here are some common prep tasks for workshops of this type:

▶ Ask each person to bring an example of a recent project that went very well, and three reasons why they believe it did, as well as an example of a project that did not go as well as hoped, and three reasons why.

▶ Do an online survey with the wider team, customers, stakeholders or among the workshop participants only, to get anonymous and therefore candid answers about what works well and what needs to be improved.

▶ Commission a third party to do telephone interviews with your main clients, stakeholders or staff, so that those interviewed can fully express themselves but won't be directly quoted. The third party then presents the results in the workshop, analysing the interviews for the main themes and keeping the names of who said what confidential.

SWOT tool

A SWOT analysis (Strengths, Weaknesses, Opportunities, Threats) is a great tool to use in workshops to help a team to work better together. This is a commonly used business tool invented by management consultant Albert Humphrey in the 1960s to help companies do better long-term planning. Because many people are familiar with this tool, it can make them feel a little more comfortable.

The four quadrants serve as a useful group analysis task.

1 Put up four flipcharts, labelled Strengths, Weaknesses, Opportunities and Threats.

2 Make sure to define each box very specifically according to the workshop objective, for example:

▶ What are the strengths of the way we currently work?

▶ What are the weaknesses in the way we currently work?

> What are the opportunities we could create if we change the way we work for the better?

> What are the threats to our team if we do not change the way we work for the better?

3 Ask each person in the group to write, without discussion and on a separate Post-it for every thought, as many different answers to each of the four questions that they can.

4 Ask them to stick these answers on the flipcharts, in the correct box.

5 Split the team into four pre-assigned groups, giving each team just one quadrant to work on (strengths, weaknesses, opportunities or threats). Consider putting more critical team members in the strengths and opportunities teams, and the more optimistic people in the weaknesses and threats teams, to make sure they are thinking from other people's perspectives, not just their own.

6 Ask each team to read through all the Post-its in their quadrant and theme them, labelling each theme and presenting those back. The team will then recognise what the major issues are, because of the visual nature of the theming. The bigger themes are probably the bigger issues – for example, if 10 people have contributed notes about getting a new computer system in the opportunities section, and just one person has requested fruit at work, the computer system is probably a more important issue.

7 Then split the team into new groups of four, each taking away one of the now themed posters (strengths, opportunities, weaknesses and threats) and ask each group to come up with ten new ideas for improving the way they work, based on that poster alone. Instead of getting everybody to think about all four and come up with ideas, it's much better to get small teams focused on a smaller number of themes, to create higher-quality ideas, rather than getting everyone to read everything.

Past, present, future tool

This tool helps people face the possibilities of the future rather than being stuck in the past. It helps to turn the present into the past, recodes the present to be a better way of working, then gives some inspiration for what the future might bring.

Basically you treat the current way of working as already over and move onto the better way, using the workshop as the day to mark this change.

1 Set up a template that lists the past, present and future in three columns.

2 In small groups, ask the teams to write down in column 1 the five main ways of working that we now agree belong in the past, starting with sentences like 'the old way of doing things was…', 'the way things used to be was…', 'the way we used to feel was…', 'this company used to be known as…', framing everything in the past tense that might be in the present.

3 Once those have been defined, ask the team to look optimistically into the future and make some ambitious changes to each element of the past, using sentences such as 'the way we will be is…', 'the future is different because…' Translate the past into the future in column 3, making sure you use language like 'when we are…' or 'we will be…' and avoid any 'if's to make sure it sounds as though it will definitely happen.

4 Then ask teams to fill in the present, as a bridge between the past and the future, answering the question: 'What will we do today to make the future happen?' This column becomes the ideas to inspire new ways of working immediately.

A: Past	C: Present	B: Future
We were always stressed because we were working on too many projects at once.	We now set a limit on the number of projects each person can do, and they will drop one project if another is more urgent.	Each person will work on the correct number of projects to be productive without being overwhelmed.
We forgot to set expectations at the beginning of projects and so we didn't always work in the same direction.	We now have a set of questions we will all answer before the project starts to make sure we understand each other's expectations.	Before any project starts we will all agree the expectations we have for each other and the project.
We forgot to plan ahead for big events and ended up being under-staffed.	We now look back over the last year to see where the pressure points were, and work out if there are similar events likely to happen in the next six months.	We will plan six months ahead in regular monthly meetings to prepare ourselves for spikes in resourcing levels.
We didn't give difficult feedback when people weren't behaving well towards each other.	We now have an agreed way of working with each other, including respect, dealing with issues and providing feedback.	We will set behavioural expectations for every member of the team, with zero tolerance for bullying or unprofessional behaviour.
We stopped having regular team meetings.	We now meet every week, even if some people can't make it.	We will meet weekly no matter what.

Working better workshop plan (4-hour workshop)

Time	Task
09.00	▶ Welcome + objective + reminder of creative behaviours
09.10	▶ Participants introduce themselves and briefly describe their prep task (examples of projects that went well or not so well recently and reasons why), writing on separate Post-its the three reasons for each
	▶ Collect the Post-its and theme them onto several flipcharts, giving each theme a name
09.30	▶ Present the results of the survey or interviews with staff, customers or shareholders, asking people to write notes as they listen
	▶ Present the SWOT tool, asking people to refer to their notes from the survey and fill out as many strengths, weaknesses, opportunities and threats as possible individually and without discussion
	▶ Split the team into four pre-assigned groups, giving each group either strengths, weaknesses, opportunities or threats to summarise and present back
	▶ Teams present back their themes from the SWOT tool
	▶ Back in their teams, they then use those themes to create at least five new ideas for better ways of working
11.00	▶ Break
11.15	▶ Split the team into groups of three, giving each team just one theme from the prep task themes (from the introductions exercise)
	▶ Introduce the past, present and future tool and ask each team to fill this out for the prep task theme, then use the tool as inspiration to create at least five new ideas for how to work better together
	▶ Each group presents their ideas back
11.45	▶ Workshop leader reminds the team of the workshop objective and criteria for choosing new ways of working
	▶ Teams each read all the statements, language and stimuli from the workshop so far and use the identifying initiatives tool (from Chapter 22) to each create one new initiative for working better
	▶ These are presented back and, if appropriate, the team vote on their favourite initiatives
12.00	▶ Workshop leader introduces the accountability tool (from Chapter 22) and asks team members to work on the actions and next steps for each of the main initiatives
	▶ Teams present these back
12.45	▶ Workshop leader talks through next steps and actions to define the final purpose statement
	▶ Closing comments from each team member
13.00	▶ Workshop ends

Ask yourself

▶ How can we prepare people to be ready to discuss any issues?

▶ How can we identify the main things we need to improve as a team?

▶ How can we use the team's ideas to make them more committed to the change?

CHAPTER TWENTY-FIVE

Influencing senior leadership positively

Use for: managing senior people in a workshop

Leading your leaders in a workshop can be difficult because you don't automatically have authority over them. Even if they ask you to lead, people in positions of authority can find it hard to participate as collaborative partners without using their status to influence others. As workshop leaders we need to flatten the hierarchy in order to get the best possible collaboration from everyone in the room.

The workshop objective: to engage senior leaders in a workshop and make them contribute towards the objective

The workshop leader needs to find a careful balance between giving senior people a voice and preventing them from taking over.

Before inviting leaders to a workshop, check with them your expectations of how they should behave, making some of these points to check they are able to participate:

▶ We will run a very structured session, and there will be regular break-out working groups that will need your full attention. You will need to take part in these – you will not be able to float or observe. We will need you there for the whole session.

▶ We will ask you not to use your phone, tablet or laptop during the session.

▶ Everyone attending the workshop, including you, will be asked to do a prep task for adding inspiration to the workshop.

▶ We want to make this as collaborative as possible, which means making sure everyone is heard, so you will be given an equal amount of time to talk as the other people in the workshop.

▶ We will be creating lots of ideas during the workshop, many of which won't be quite right at first. We will not be evaluating these until later, so that we can create many options to choose from. It is important that you allow these ideas to be created before commenting on them.

▶ No decisions will be made in the workshop, but you will have full involvement in any decisions that are made as a result of the workshop.

If your seniors won't meet these expectations, invite them instead to feed in their views in advance and receive the workshop outputs afterwards.

Prep tasks for senior leaders

Like every workshop, you will make the most of your time and collect important inputs by asking for a prep task to be done in advance by each person attending.

Prep tasks for senior leaders can be more business related, rather than too creative or personal. Always make sure they are asked to bring a positive angle, even if you are inviting any concerns to be expressed.

For example:

▶ Consider the main opportunity for this project and the main risk, and be prepared to share these at the workshop.

▶ Bring an example of a brand or company that has faced challenges like yours and succeeded, and be ready to explain how they were successful.

▶ Be ready to say one thing you want the workshop to achieve, and one thing you do not want to happen or come out of the workshop.

Making an impact with senior leaders

Consider how to work with senior leaders so that they feel they have an influence on the direction of the project, without overwhelming them with so many details that they become distracted or go off point.

Leaders are often extremely busy, so you have to make use of their time effectively by structuring the information they receive, how they contribute their views and what they do with this information.

It is therefore important that you present the topic to them with impact, so that they get to engage and focus their attention on the objectives, and be clear what you want them to do with this information.

Making an impact with information

Meet real people

▶ It's all very well telling leaders about their customers, but having them meet these customers face to face can have a considerable impact. Arrange home visits to consumers' houses before the workshop, or bring customers to the session and have them participate throughout, contributing their thoughts and ideas as equal participants.

▶ For example, in a toothpaste project we took global marketing directors and scientists to visit Indian consumers in Delhi to understand how they stored and used toothbrushes and toothpaste. Many of the team members had no idea what it was like in an average Indian home, and soon realised how water scarcity, communal basins and poverty were huge issues affecting how often people were able to brush their teeth.

Give bite-sized information

▶ Whether you present your topic as infographics, collages, playing cards or in a diagram, make the main points quickly and make them memorable. Get to the point early, then allow time for detail and discussion. Leaders tend to want the whole picture or context before leaping in with ideas.

▶ For example, on a future trends project for a beverages company, we gave away a pack of five cards that represented the five main trends that were going to have an impact on the company in the next 10 years. When materials are specially designed and printed, people are reluctant to throw them away, and so you and your project will stay at the forefront of their minds if they carry those cards with them.

Challenge them

▶ Senior people are used to being agreed with. Consider appropriate ways of testing their knowledge, identifying their stereotypes, understanding their biases in order to get them thinking. Like the myth buster tool, being a bit controversial at first will make them remember what they learned later.

▶ For example, giving a short multiple-choice test about the topic before giving participants the answers can make people excited and more receptive to what they will learn once they have been given the answers.

Delight them

▶ Everyone loves to be pleasantly surprised, so going a little further in your preparation can make all the difference. Have an unexpectedly lovely invitation sent to them, give away small gifts that are relevant to the workshop topic and inspire discussion, or send them on an enjoyable lunchtime break.

▶ For example, I often hold workshops near Borough Market in London, and no matter what the topic, it's a great energiser to send team members out into the market, with a little pack containing a map, some money and some information about the history of the area, and perhaps a treasure hunt task or product to find. You can always make this relevant to the topic in some way, or simply use it as an energiser.

Tell them something new

▶ People love to be able to tell their friends or colleagues about something new and interesting. Whether it's a personal story they hear and want to repeat, or a new fad that's happening with younger people, or the latest technology – it all becomes currency to share with others.

▶ Ban examples that everyone already knows. For instance, if I'm preparing stimuli for how to make people change their habits, I won't refer to well-known examples (such as how Apple changed the music industry) because they are so familiar now it doesn't feel new. I look for interesting, local and unusual stories about brands or businesses that are clever and different – for example, the 'Save the flush, pee in the shower' campaign in Brazil that encouraged people to pee in the shower to save the water used by flushing (sponsored by a Brazilian non-profit dedicated to saving the rainforest). Tell them a story they will want to repeat to others.

Making an impact

I was working on a soft drinks project in the Middle East, and we were looking for ways of increasing the sales of a powdered soft drink already popular across the region. In the rest of the region a 500g pack was selling well, but not in Egypt. The marketing director and I went to visit Egyptian women in their homes to understand what drinks they were buying for their families and why.

We visited a woman and talked with her about her life, her husband and children, how she shopped for products and how she fed her family. We asked to look inside her fridge and found that it contained a cabbage, a half-empty bottle of cola, a bottle of water and a banana. She had some dried beans and other dry goods on the table next to the fridge, and that was all. We were surprised, and asked her how she fed her family with this amount of food. She explained that her husband was paid at the end of each day. He would bring the money home, and the next morning she would go to buy exactly the right amount of food for that day.

A 500g pack of powdered soft drink that would last a month might have been good value to her in theory, but it was an impossible investment when she was buying everything daily. This led us to think about how to produce smaller pack sizes for more frequent purchases.

Talk like me tool

This is a great way to challenge and surprise senior leaders. Talk like me makes people think on behalf of their customer, then shows them how close they were to the truth, leaving them more able to understand their customers' perspectives.

1 Before the workshop, recruit some customers, one per workshop team member, and create for each customer a small outline of who they are, for example first name, gender, age, job and family situation.

2   Invite them to attend the workshop, but keep this secret from the team.

3   In your workshop, give out a customer card to each member of the team, making sure to mix them to be as unfamiliar as possible to each individual (e.g. give the profile card of an older woman to a younger man, give a teenager card to a woman without children, etc.).

4   Give your team members five minutes to read through their card and to imagine who this person is, what their life is like, what they love, what they are worried about and, of course, how they feel about your product.

5   Seat the team in a circle (no more than five people per group, so split into more circles depending on numbers) and ask them to pretend to be the customer on their card for a focus group.

6   Moderate the discussion like a focus group, asking them first to introduce themselves (which they will do quite easily), then about their lives, and then go into more detail about the workshop topic. Don't ask more than about 10 questions. So for example:

▶   What do you do for a living?

▶   Can you tell us about your family?

▶   How would you describe your life?

▶   What was your happiest memory?

▶   What are the things that make you happiest now?

▶   What do you sometimes worry about?

▶   Do you currently use our products?

▶   Why do you choose them instead of our competitors' products?

▶   Are there any real advantages to using our products?

▶   Is there anything you would like to see improved in our products?

7   As the team members role play, they quite quickly use up the information they have about the customer and begin to have to create the answers based on what they think they know. As they progress, they will know some answers and not others, but will try to answer them to the best of their ability. This can expose incorrect assumptions and stereotypes.

8   Bring the focus group to a close, asking team members to make notes to themselves about anything that occurred to them during the focus group.

9   Finally, surprise the team by asking the real customers to come in and have them sit in the same chairs as their impersonators sat.

The moderator then runs the focus group again, with the same questions, which the real customers hear for the first time and have to answer honestly.

10 Because they all had to answer the same questions, the team members will listen intently to what their customer says. Whether or not they got some answers right, the tool will help to contrast what they now know with what they got wrong.

To make it less challenging, you can change this tool to run like a game show by preparing some consumer questions and answers in advance, asking team members to guess the answers that were given before revealing what the customers actually said. Alternatively, you could video some customer responses and pause them to let the team guess what they said before revealing each answer.

Four futures tool

To motivate senior leadership to do something different or create some ideas, a visioning tool works well. Senior leaders are used to looking at the big picture, and want to influence the future.

This tool helps them to create personally resonant scenarios of a successful future, and inspires ideas for how to achieve that success.

1 Ask the team to consider the future, in five years' time, when this project has been a huge success. Give them a couple of minutes to think about what it would feel like in that future.

2 After allowing a little time for self-reflection, show the team the four futures template. The workshop leader should have prepared the exact wording of these questions to suit the workshop topic, within these four quadrants:

   ▶ What does this success look like at work?
   ▶ What does this success look like at home?
   ▶ What does this success look like to customers?
   ▶ What does this success look like to competitors?

3 Ask the team members to each write at least one answer per question on a Post-it note, in full, descriptive and emotional sentences, and then to stick their answers in the relevant quadrant.

4 Split the team members into four groups, assigning one group to each quadrant, and ask each group to read through the Post-its and select the best ones (3–5) to read back to the team.

5 The groups present back their best examples from each quadrant.

6 After presenting, the teams can spend some time creating ideas for how to achieve that future vision.

In five years' time, when this project is hugely successful, what will the president of the company say at the Christmas party about this working team?	In five years' time, when this project is amazingly successful, what will you tell your family or friends about your role in this project?
This team transformed our entire business in the last five years. We are now the leaders of our industry, and it is all down to them!	I love my job because it gives me the chance to create really new products that make people's lives better.
When this project is incredibly successful, what will you overhear people saying to each other about your company in the supermarket?	What will you hear your competitors saying about you in five years' time when this project is wildly successful?
You must try this product – you will wonder why it took you so long to stop using the old one.	Can we try to copy them, or are we now too far behind?

Four futures

Influencing senior leadership workshop plan (4-hour workshop)

Time	Task
09.00	▶ Welcome + objective + reminder of creative behaviours
09.10	▶ Participants introduce themselves and briefly describe their prep task (top three opportunities for this project), writing the three points on separate Post-its ▶ The workshop leader collects each person's comments, sticking them up on a wall to refer to later
09.30	▶ Run a 'talk like me' exercise, bringing in target customers at the end to hear their answers ▶ Encourage questions and discussion afterwards between the leaders and customers

Time	Task
10.30	▶ Break and let the customers leave
11.00	▶ Workshop leader splits people into groups of three
	▶ Ask each group to reflect on their talk like me exercise and create some ideas for the project based on that experience
	▶ Each group presents their ideas back
11.15	▶ Workshop leader splits team into new groups of three, making sure everyone works with someone new for this last round
	▶ Give each team a four futures template and one of the themes from the prep work task to complete and present back to the team
	▶ Each group then uses the completed four futures as inspiration to create some new ideas for the project
	▶ Each team presents their ideas back
12.15	▶ Workshop leader reminds the team of the workshop objective and criteria for choosing ways forward
	▶ Team members read all the ideas from the workshop, each completing an identifying initiatives tool
	▶ These are presented back and the team vote on their favourite initiatives to move forward with
12.45	▶ Split into final teams, one per initiative, and complete an accountability template for each, presenting them back
	▶ Workshop leader talks through next steps and actions
	▶ Closing comments from each team member
13.00	▶ Workshop ends

Ask yourself

▶ How can you impress and surprise these people?

▶ How can you make this the most memorable workshop they have been to?

▶ What do we want them to do as a result of this workshop?

26

Positive turnaround

Use for: turning a negative situation into a positive one

People can be very emotional about projects that have gone wrong, and that can affect the confidence and motivation of a team. It is important to be sympathetic to the level of emotion that the team feel, but as a workshop leader, be careful not to get dragged into a pessimistic place along with them.

The workshop objective: to recognise what has happened and move on positively

In negative situations, there is a danger of spending too long looking at the issue, defining the problem and revelling in the negatives. If the problem owner unburdens all their troubles, the people who are listening can find themselves stuck in a similar way of thinking and limited by exactly the same constraints.[1]

Resist the temptation to define the problem deeply. Rather, keep the solution providers at a distance from the problems so that they can still offer some solutions to get out. This means balancing an understanding of the issue with new inspiration, in order to create ways forward.

The causes of a negative situation

Whatever the negative situation, it is crucial to identify the reasons behind the negative situation, rather than focusing on the results of that situation.

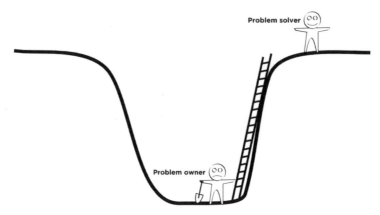

Digging a hole

For example:

▶ If a business has lost market share, focus on working out the reasons that led to that loss, such as competitor launches, distribution problems or poor advertising.

▶ If a team has received poor customer service feedback, focus on why their performance was so poor, for instance high workload, lack of training, no rewards for good feedback.

Time is more valuably spent working out what led to this circumstance and therefore what can lead us out of it. In my experience, irrespective of the industry or organisation, there are some common issues that seem to contribute to a negative situation:

▶ The team didn't communicate enough with each other.

▶ Workloads are too high for us to cope.

▶ Expectations for the project are different across the team.

▶ We are not working efficiently together.

▶ We have not evolved and improved as a business.

▶ Competitors have changed the rules or taken our business.

▶ Our customers are changing and we are not keeping up.

A general rule for workshops like this is to spend a third of the time defining and expressing the issue and two thirds turning the situation in a positive direction or towards positive solutions.

Reasons why tool

An easy way to begin a workshop like this is with the reasons why tool. Ask the team to come prepared to answer these two questions:

▶ Can you think of a project or initiative you worked on that went really well recently, and three reasons why you believe it went so well?

▶ Can you think of a situation or project you worked on recently that did not go well, and be ready to share three reasons why you believe it did not go as well as it should have?

You can ask for these answers in advance as a prep task or ask the participants to be ready to discuss them within the session. Crucially, they are focusing on the positives, not just the negatives. And, just as importantly, they are not focusing on the situation itself, they are focusing on the reasons behind it.

Theme the answers into groups, giving each group a name. With the themes on the wall, it then becomes easy to see what the big issues are, because the size of the theme will show the most common points mentioned. Often the themes immediately lend themselves to inspiring new ideas.

Here are some ways to then activate the themes:

▶ Ask the right question: take the theme and turn it into a constructive question. For example, if there is a theme called 'poor communication between team members', this leads us to ask, 'what can we do to improve communication?' or 'how can we have excellent communication between members in future?' and generate ideas on that theme.

▶ More or less: each team takes one positive theme and asks, 'how can we make this happen more?', and one negative theme and asks, 'how can we make this happen less?'

Dos and don'ts tool

Once you have found the reasons why things go well or badly, think about applying them to some difficult projects to stress test them on real scenarios.

1 Ask people to write down a list of dos and don'ts, on a separate Post-it for each point. Their points should relate to 'this is what we will do to avoid this negative situation in future' and 'this is what we won't do, so that we can avoid this negative situation in future'.

2 Gather all the dos and don'ts and split the team into two groups, one group summarising the main dos and the other the main don'ts. These become your guiding principles for how to work to avoid this negative situation in future.

3 Split the team into three groups, giving each group a realistic or common scenario that they are likely to face in future that could potentially become negative.

4 Ask them to use the dos and don'ts principles to work through that scenario, and see if they can prevent the situation from becoming negative.

5 As a result of this exercise, teams improve wording or add to the dos and don'ts principles.

6 For example, we agree one don't is: 'Don't take on more work than you can manage.' Give that team a realistic scenario that might apply, such as 'my boss asks me to take on a big important project for our main client'. Work out how to take on this task but still not take on more work than you can manage, perhaps by deprioritising another project.

Old way, new way tool

Another way to encourage the team to put aside an old way of working is to ask them to tell a story about the old way versus the new way, using some realistic scenarios.

▶ Define the realistic scenario first, again: 'My boss asks me to take on a big important project for our main client.'

▶ Ask teams to tell a story about what would have happened in the old way. For example, 'When my boss asked me to take on a big important project for our main client, I felt I couldn't let her down and so I said yes, even though I was already overworked on my other projects. I then had to cancel a big family gathering I'd organised and worked all weekend to complete this new project on time. I delivered the project perfectly, but then had to take a week off work for a stress-related illness.'

▶ Then ask them to retell the story in the new way of working. For example, 'When my boss asked me to take on a big important project for our main client, I explained that I didn't want to let her down and would love to work on the new project. However, I told her I would need to change the delivery dates of my other projects to take on this one. I also told her I had an important family gathering over the weekend and so would start the work on Monday. She agreed, and we delivered the important project a few days late but done very well. I then completed all my other projects.'

▶ After each team presents their old story and new story, they then create new ideas or commitments to turn the situation into a positive one.

The story of the old way is therapeutic because everybody gets all their frustration out and they can discuss people and scenarios that they know will happen, in a constructive way. The new stories are fun and inspiring, and allow you to create an ideal scenario as the main thing you remember (rather than the old way). Each leads to new ideas for how to turn the situation around.

Positive turnaround workshop plan (4-hour workshop)

Time	Task
09.00	▶ Welcome + objective + reminder of creative behaviours
09.10	▶ Participants introduce themselves and briefly describe their prep task (the project that went well and three reasons why, and the project that did not go well and three reasons why), writing on separate Post-its the three reasons for each
	▶ The workshop leader collects the Post-its and themes them
09.30	▶ Split the team into smaller groups and ask them each to work on one positive and one negative theme
	▶ Each group turns their themes into constructive questions and uses these to create three ideas for turning the situation into a positive one
	▶ Teams present back their ideas to each other
10.15	▶ Break
10.30	▶ Workshop leader splits team into new groups of three, making sure everyone works with someone new
	▶ Ask the group to individually create some dos and don'ts for keeping the situation positive in future
	▶ Workshop leader collects these and splits the team into two, one to summarise the dos and one to summarise the don'ts
	▶ Each group presents their dos/don'ts back

▶

Time	Task
11.00	▶ Workshop leader splits team into three new groups, making sure everyone works with someone new for this last round
	▶ Give each group a realistic scenario to work with, asking them to prepare to tell the old story and the new story about this scenario
	▶ Teams present back their old and new stories
	▶ Each group then uses those stories for three new ideas to ensure future situations are positive, not negative
	▶ Each group presents their ideas back
12.00	▶ Workshop leader reminds the team of the workshop objective and criteria for choosing positive new directions or solutions
	▶ Teams each read all the statements, language and stimuli from the workshop so far, and using the identifying initiatives tool, individually suggest an initiative to turn the situation into a positive
	▶ These are presented back and, if appropriate, the team vote on their favourite initiatives for further development
12.45	▶ Workshop leader talks through next steps and actions
	▶ Closing comments from each team member
13.00	▶ Workshop ends

Ask yourself

▶ What do people need to express about what went wrong before they can move on?

▶ How can we make sure that the ways forward we create will stand up to real-life scenarios?

▶ How can we make people feel better at the end than they did at the start of the workshop?

27

Team updates

> **Use for:** getting several different teams to share learning and updates
>
> For teams who work in different regions or offices, it is important to update and reconnect with each other regularly. These update meetings are vital for building relationships, setting common goals and sharing learning and inspiration across the business. However, because these meetings happen infrequently, we pack them full of presentations and updates and leave no time for discussions and debates.
>
> Many update sessions follow an agenda of team members presenting to each other over the course of a day. It is common to run out of time, or for one person to run over on time and so have to rush those items last on the agenda. Because there is so much presenting and passive listening, people can get bored or tired and retreat to check emails.

> **The workshop objective:** to use face-to-face time to create outputs, not just updates
>
> If you have face-to-face time only every six months or once a year, think carefully about what you want that time to be spent on. Certainly updates need to be shared, but would the time in the session be better used if people could spend more time discussing rather than being presented to?

Pre-read tasks

Doing some updating in advance of the session means you can maximise the face-to-face time for discussion, rather than using it up in updates.

169

It is common to send out 'pre-reads', shorthand for some reading to do before a big meeting, to get everyone up to date. It is also common for people to read the pre-read on the way to the meeting or just as the meeting starts, or not at all, so pre-reads are generally not effective.

However, a structured pre-read task can be effective because it makes sure that people do the reading.

Here are some ways to make sure pre-reads get done:

▶ **Make it exciting.** Make them want to do it. Create the pre-read in the form of a glossy magazine that you deliver to their desk a week beforehand, or create a short video with the main learning points brought to life, posing some controversial questions to have in their heads. Tell them there will be a test on the pre-read and they can win a prize. Anything you can do to get people curious and excited in advance is a good idea because it will save time on the day.

▶ **Produce a podcast.** Record the presentation and send that in advance, so people can get the update and presentation in their own time and at their own convenience, rather than using the time in the session to listen to it. To make sure people listen, ask them to come ready to tell the team their most interesting insights or with key questions to discuss face to face.

▶ **Ask for answers.** Send out a pre-read and ask people to send you answers to three questions as a result of that pre-read, for example:

    ▶ What was the most interesting part of the update deck that you'd like to discuss more in the meeting?

    ▶ Do you have any specific questions that you want clarified on the day?

    ▶ What are the main opportunities that all the teams share and could work on together in the meeting?

▶ **Divide the pre-read.** Give everyone one specific thing to read, rather than the whole document. If there's a lot to read, getting everyone to read everything often dilutes any understanding as people's attention is spread too thin.

Avoid cognitive overload

Scientists have studied fish to understand how a school of fish can make better decisions together than a single fish can on its own.[1] One of the advantages of being in a school of fish is that your attention is focused on a very specific area, because you can't see beyond that space due to the other fish around you. This means that every fish has all its attention focused on one area and can immediately pick up changes in that small space. We can adopt the same thinking to avoid cognitive overload. It is better to get each person to focus on one specific space rather than everyone trying to understand everything.

Structure the sharing

Structure what people are sharing and how they share it. If you have a one-day update meeting, in most cases you should spend only half a day updating each other and then spend the other half connecting and creating.

Here are some ways to structure sharing and save time for collaborating:

▶ **Set a time limit.** Tell all speakers that they have 10 minutes. Warn them they will be stopped after 10 minutes, and advise them to rehearse with this in mind. Some people think that if they present really fast they can get a lot across in 10 minutes, and this can be quite uncomfortable to watch. So if you're setting a time limit, set a slide limit, too. On PowerPoint slides, I allow 3–5 minutes per slide. So for 10 minutes, I'd set a maximum of three slides. An added benefit is that it is energising for everyone involved, as there's usually a bit of a laugh when the 10-minute alarm goes off, and it's far more enjoyable to listen to a series of 10-minute presentations than half-hour presentations.

▶ **Questions at the end.** Another way to save time is to limit questions and discussions until a certain point in the day. Ask for questions and discussion points to be written down during the presentations on separate Post-its, which will be collected and themed by the workshop leader, and answered in turn later.

▶ **A speaking template.** Give each speaker the same template so that everyone answers the same questions, in the same format, in the same order. This means that the information being received is clear and easy to listen to. It also means the speaker has to adapt their presentation to the objective, rather than using a presentation they wrote a while ago. For example:

   ▶ Slide 1: 'What's happened in my market since we last saw each other'

   ▶ Slide 2: 'What our competitors are doing'

   ▶ Slide 3: 'What our next directions will be'

   Other slide templates you could ask for are:

   ▶ 'Projects we are most proud of'

   ▶ 'Things that we wish we had made but our competitors beat us to it'

   ▶ 'Mistakes that we have learned from this year'

   ▶ 'Opportunities that we would like to make use of next year'

   ▶ 'If I could wish for anything else I would…'

   ▶ 'If I could look into the future I'd want to know…'

▶ **Collect ideas to theme.** Have the participants write their questions, ideas and challenges on separate Post-its to stick up on the wall under relevant headings ('ideas', 'questions', etc.). This encourages people to actively listen, writing notes as they talk, keeping them engaged. Collect the Post-its regularly during each talk, to remind people that they should keep writing.

What advice would you give yourself?

I ran a project for TV producers to learn from digital and social media experts. We asked each speaker to prepare just one slide, answering the question: 'What advice would I give today to the person I was 10 years ago?' Because each speaker was well ahead of the audience in digital media, the advice they gave themselves was immediate advice that the TV people could use. The constraint of one slide made the speakers clever and creative with their answers.

Team update workshop plan (6-hour workshop)

Time	Task
09.00	▶ Welcome + objective + reminder of creative behaviours
09.10	▶ Participants introduce themselves with job titles, roles, etc.
09.30	▶ Workshop leader introduces speaker 1, reminding people to make notes under the headings on the wall (ideas, questions, etc.) ▶ Speaker 1 talks for 10 minutes ▶ Workshop leader collects Post-its and adds them to the wall, theming as they go
09.45	▶ Workshop leader introduces speaker 2, reminding people to make notes under the headings on the wall (ideas, questions, etc.) ▶ Speaker 2 talks for 10 minutes ▶ Workshop leader collects Post-its and adds them to the wall, theming as they go
10.00	▶ Workshop leader introduces speaker 3, reminding people to make notes under the headings on the wall (ideas, questions, etc.) ▶ Speaker 3 talks for 10 minutes ▶ Workshop leader collects Post-its and adds them to the wall, theming as they go
10.15	▶ Break
10.30	▶ Workshop leader introduces speaker 4, reminding people to make notes under the headings on the wall (ideas, questions, etc.) ▶ Speaker 4 talks for 10 minutes ▶ Workshop leader collects Post-its and adds them to the wall, theming as they go
10.45	▶ Workshop leader introduces speaker 5, reminding people to make notes under the headings on the wall (ideas, questions, etc.) ▶ Speaker 5 talks for 10 minutes ▶ Workshop leader collects Post-its and adds them to the wall, theming as they go
11.00	▶ Workshop leader introduces speaker 6, reminding people to make notes under the headings on the wall (ideas, questions, etc.) ▶ Speaker 6 talks for 10 minutes ▶ Workshop leader collects Post-its and adds them to the wall, theming as they go
11.15	▶ Break ▶ Workshop leader finalises themes on the wall and prepares group names for next section
11.30	▶ Workshop leader splits team into pre-selected groups of three ▶ Show the team all the Post-it notes from the morning, under each heading ▶ Ask each group to take away one section (e.g. one group takes the ideas, one takes the questions, etc.) and summarise the main points for the rest of the group ▶ Each group presents their summarised themes back to the group
12.00	▶ Workshop leader explains the work to be done in the afternoon ▶ Before breaking for lunch, ask each team member to say one thing they found useful from the morning updates, writing these down as they are said ▶ Break for lunch

173

Time	Task
12.30	▶ Lunch ▶ Workshop leader considers how to input morning thinking into afternoon session
13.00	▶ This section would be designed in advance by the workshop leader to maximise the face-to-face time people have and the specific needs of that team. For example: ▶ Continue the conversations from the morning, turning them into some initiatives using the identifying initiatives tool ▶ An expert speaker and/or customers could join for co-creation ▶ Teams could split into smaller groups for other update meetings ▶ You could lead a quick ideas session for innovations ▶ You could lead a working better together session for the team
14.45	▶ Workshop leader talks through next steps and actions ▶ Closing comments from each team member
15.00	▶ Workshop ends

Ask yourself

▶ How can we avoid boring people with too many presentations?

▶ How can we leave space in the agenda for people to use the updates to create ideas?

▶ How can we keep the energy levels high throughout?

▶ How can we use collective intelligence in the update day?

28

Team building

Use for: leading a team-building workshop

Traditional team-building activities such as clay pigeon shooting or bridge building might be fun, but they don't always have a lasting impact on how team members work together in the future. Workshops are great for team building because they provide a space for people to work together in new ways towards an output.

The workshop objective: helping a team learn more about each other by working collaboratively

Team-building workshops can have any objective, so long as the team are working collaboratively to create something. Here are some common team-building objectives:

- ▶ To improve how we work together.
- ▶ To improve relationships between two departments.
- ▶ To work together on some ideas for the future.
- ▶ To learn from each other.
- ▶ To understand each other's roles.
- ▶ To plan our social calendar for the year.
- ▶ To get to know each other better.

Time to meet and connect

The main difference from other workshops is that you allow more time for people to meet, chat and get to know each other. So while the time is structured, the pace is more relaxed and the atmosphere should feel a bit lighter. Start by inviting everyone to come early but allow them the chance to have breakfast together. Make sure you mix teams so that people work with different colleagues from those they normally do. Allow an hour or even more for lunch. Make sure you plan into the day some sort of early evening slot with some socialising time, drinks and snacks, or even dinner so that people can end the day on a high.

Ideal job tool

One of my favourite exercises for getting to know people is to ask everyone to describe, without constraints, their ideal job and what they would love to spend their time doing (other than their current jobs, of course!).

1 Warn the team before the day that you will ask them this question. To make it more playful, ask them to bring a picture or a drawing of them in their ideal job, doing what they want to do.

2 When people answer, ask them to describe why they love the idea of this job so much. You will understand a lot more about everyone in the team and the values that motivate them.

3 If you want to create some stimulus for use later in the session, ask people to write the three reasons for listing that job on three separate Post-its, then collect the Post-its from everyone and divide them into themes, such as 'helping others', 'I love food' or 'travelling to new places'. Irrespective of what they are, these can become the fresh angles for ideas later in the session.

Team directory

A team directory is a great output for any team and is surprisingly useful for years afterwards.

1 Two weeks before the workshop, ask each team member to send in a photo of themselves doing something they enjoy. This does not necessarily have to be related to work, but should show their face clearly.

2 Also ask them to send in their updated details (job title, phone number, email address, etc.).

3 Finally, ask them for something funny or personal, such as how to bribe them to do you a favour (and people can then say 'biscuits' or 'just ask nicely' or 'talk to me in person'), or two truths and a lie about themselves (which can then be a point of conversation when you talk to them in the session or afterwards).

4 Produce a profile card for each person with contact details, a photo and the funny or personal detail, and give out in a booklet to everyone at the start of the workshop. This means that they can look up people they don't know or have something to talk to them about when they meet.

Team-building workshop plan (6-hour workshop)

Time	Task
09.30	▶ Team members arrive, get refreshments and name tags ▶ Workshop leader introduces themselves to each participant ▶ Check whether prep task has been done and, if not, ask each person to complete it before the workshop begins
09.45	▶ Breakfast served and team chat with each other
10.00	▶ Welcome ▶ Introduce the objective ▶ Reminder of the creative behaviours ▶ Start with a little bit of a review of the last year and the main plans for the next year, or a quick company update ▶ Remind the team that this time is an investment in them and their working ways and so they should really enjoy themselves and participate as fully as possible
10.30	▶ Participants introduce themselves and briefly describe their prep task (bringing a picture or a drawing of themselves in their ideal job, doing what they would like to do) ▶ Ask them to write the three reasons for that job on three separate Post-its ▶ Collect the Post-its from everyone, theming where people have put similar thoughts, such as 'helping others', 'I love food' or 'travelling to new places'
11.00	▶ Put people into smaller, pre-arranged groups that mix them up and have them working with someone from a different department ▶ Introduce the sculpture competition tool, asking people to produce a model of what their ideal office would look like ▶ Give each team a variety of materials – one team Play-Doh, one K'NEX, one pipe cleaners and one Duplo ▶ Ask teams to present back their piece and take note of the language they use to describe their ideal office ▶ Ask teams to create some new ideas for the office inspired by the sculptures

Time	Task
11.45	▶ Break
12.00	▶ Have a motivating talk from an expert, or survey about the team, or presentation of customer insights
	▶ People take notes as they listen and ask questions
13.00	▶ Lunch
	▶ Arrange a seating plan so different people meet each other
14.00	▶ Workshop leader splits team into new groups of three, making sure everyone works with someone new for this last round
	▶ If it is team building between two departments, get people from the different departments to pair up with each other
	▶ In small teams, take the original themes from the introductory exercise and combine them with the themes from the sculpture round and the inspiration from the expert talk to come up with some ideas for better ways of working together in the future
	▶ This might be something to do with new ideas for projects, or it might just be about creating some new initiatives for the next year
	▶ Teams present back their ideas, along with plans for how to make them happen
15.00	▶ Workshop leader reminds the team of the different parts of the day so far, and how the ideas and initiatives will be taken forward
	▶ End by asking people to go around the room voicing their commitments to highlight what they will do more of, or less of, and what they will do differently in their future jobs
	▶ Here you could ask them to write a letter to themselves, using the 'note to self' tool
15.30	▶ Workshop ends. Invite everyone back for 6pm drinks and dinner together

Ask yourself

▶ How can we use people's time productively and enjoyably?

▶ How can you enable people to get to know colleagues they don't work with every day?

▶ How can we structure the day to end on a positive note?

29

Regular team meetings

Use for: regular team meetings

Regular team meetings are necessary, but due to time pressure and a lack of preparation, they can become a repetitive list of project updates instead of a positive use of collaboration time. Whether face to face or on a conference call, you can still plan to use more of the live time for discussion, debates and ideas.

The workshop objective: to make regular updates more dynamic and collaborative

Work out the essential information that the team need to update each other on, and develop a clear and simple template to use to do this. When updates are purely verbal, they are also less structured, can go off the point and are not comparable with each other.

Consider a one-pager for each project or person updating, which outlines the main points to make it easy to read in advance, and then only the 'requiring approval, action or advice' section needs to be discussed in the meeting itself.

Project name	Cactus (shampoo)
Actions, advice or approval needed	Approval of budget for new qualitative research project to explore pack design options
Current status	Stimulus in production
Timing for delivery	Christmas 2020

Key learnings	Key challenges
Make cactus the obvious extract	Stand out from other shampoos
Simple design	Saturated market
Keep advert brand consistent	Communicating ingredients in a simple way

Project one-pager

Send pre-reads and prep tasks

To make sure that the time in the meeting is spent collaborating, ask team members to read the updates in advance.

1 Ask the team to send you their update one-pagers beforehand.

2 Send out all the one-pagers in one document to everyone attending a day before the meeting. Consider the right order of the updates, making sure that similar issues or requests for advice are grouped together.

3 Ask the team to read through the status updates and be ready to discuss the points that require approval, action or advice.

4 When you run the meeting, focus on the Requiring Approval, Action or Advice box only for each project (the person who wrote the slide may want to add context, but you can make sure you focus the time on the solution, not the update). Research has shown that people tune out after just 10–15 seconds of listening to someone else,[1] so try to get the team in the habit of headlining their project at the beginning so it's very clear

what they want from the team first. This also helps people to focus on action rather than explanation.

5 If any updates are 'for info only' then do not discuss them.

Provide inspiration

Regular updates can become predictable and boring. Consider ways of not just updating people but inspiring them too. When I worked for ITV Imagine, our team was tasked with inspiring new content ideas with cultural insights, new technologies and trends. To keep up with the demand for stimulus, each team member chose a specialist topic (such as food trends, celebrity gossip, sports news) that they presented to the team once a month in rotation.

In each of our weekly update meetings we had at least two cultural inspiration presentations, as well as our project updates. The team became more and more elaborate with their presentations, bringing in guest speakers, providing food and drinks, having a dance lesson and hosting a catwalk show to bring to life some fashion trends. Of course we looked forward to our weekly team updates. But more than that, it meant our team were curious, well informed and ready with inspiration for the next creative workshop topic.

Rotate leadership

Give each team member the chance to run the update meeting in turn. Like having a guest editor for a magazine, a guest leader can think about new ways of doing things, even if the content of the update is relatively similar.

For global teams this could mean they run it in their own time zone, for example. Rotating leaders might also choose a different theme or inspiration for each meeting. It might be as simple as the guest leader choosing where to hold the meeting or what food is served. Anything that changes the energy or mixes up the way things are done is going to bring energy into regular updates.

Regular team meeting workshop plan (2-hour workshop)

Time	Task
09.00	▶ Welcome + objective + reminder of creative behaviours
09.15	▶ Give the team a quiz in order to check how well they read the updates ▶ Offer a prize to whoever wins and applaud the winner
09.20	▶ Go around the room discussing the points that require approval, action or advice for each person's one-pager (rather than reading out each update) ▶ Leader listens to discussion and, as they are talking, makes a note of solutions on Post-its and sticks them to the relevant one-pager
10.00	▶ Provide inspiration to encourage the team to engage with the theme of the update or to add richness and inspiration to each team update. For example, invite a guest speaker, provide a box full of multi-sensory stimuli, watch a film, listen to some music, eat relevant foods etc.
10.30	▶ Write a list of actions and decide who personally is going to commit to each action as a result of the session ▶ Schedule in the next update meeting and discuss what should be achieved by then ▶ Agree who will source the inspiration for the next session
11.00	▶ Team update ends

Ask yourself

▶ How can you maximise time in the session for conversation and ideas rather than verbal updates?

▶ How will we get the essential information across quickly, to spend more time discussing and collaborating?

▶ What can we use to inspire people?

▶ What can we ask people to do in advance?

▶ How will we make the meeting unpredictable, surprising or more enjoyable?

CHAPTER THIRTY
Review
workshops

Use for: reviewing lots of information and creating new ways forward

We live in a time of information obesity. It is sometimes easier to commission new research rather than reviewing what we already have. Information reviews are very important, but with too much information people can become overwhelmed and find it hard to work out how to move forward.

The workshop objective: to work as a team to understand what you already know and what your knowledge gaps are

A new approach to information reviews

Instead of the review being the responsibility of just one person, a review workshop makes use of the collective to create a shared review experience. The key to a successful information review workshop is in designing thorough prep tasks for each person attending. The prep tasks then feed into a structured review workshop.

Instead of:	A new approach:
Gathering the existing reports and reading them...	Go wider than traditional reports, for example interviewing people who are knowledgeable about the topic, desk research sources and related social media.
Just one person doing the review on behalf of the project team...	Make each person in the team responsible for reviewing a couple of reports, interviewing at least one person and doing targeted desk research.

Instead of:	A new approach:
Assigning an external consultant to review the information...	Invite external consultants to participate as team members, in order to benefit from their fresh perspectives. They each do the same type of reviews as the rest of the team.
Each person in the team reviewing their own information (scientists review the science, etc.)...	Each team member reviews their own information, in addition to the general reports, with new, fresh questions to focus on. They also share their information with someone from a different department who is also looking at it.
Everyone reviewing everything and sharing their thoughts in a meeting...	Select several reports for each person to read in detail. Make sure each report is reviewed by more than one person. Don't dilute attention by having everyone read too much.

Fresh questions tool

Once you have assigned the reports, interviews and desk research tasks to each person, ask them to review all their sources, and from that review, answer some fresh questions. For example:

▶ What are the five most important customer needs?

▶ What are the three main opportunities for this project?

▶ What are the top three challenges we need to be aware of?

▶ What are the three main trends that will affect our market in future?

Preparing for a review workshop

1 Identify the sources of information you have, including people to speak to and desk research to do.

2 Carefully design some fresh thinking questions to fit your workshop topic.

3 Assign each person some reports to read (making sure each report gets read by at least two people), a person to talk with and some desk research to do.

4 Provide a template for each person to fill in, one slide per fresh question. With the example questions above, each person will prepare four slides only, with one slide on the five most important customer needs, the next on the three main opportunities, etc. Give each person the same set of questions to answer, no matter how diverse their review sources.

5 Ask the team to send in their completed prep tasks in advance of the workshop.

6 As the workshop leader, collect all the completed fresh question templates and split them by question, so for example put all the slides from question 1 together, all the slides from question 2 together, etc.

Keep it visual

Consider how to present the reviewed information so that people can read it as soon as they walk into the workshop space. Stick up a flipchart for each question, so that people can read what everyone wrote, or, if you have more time, bring the information to life by creating posters with some of the main slides from each report and some pictures of customers.

Working out what you don't know

One of the most useful outputs of a knowledge review is identifying as a team what you don't know and what you need to find out before moving forward.

Information review

I remember doing an information review for a laundry project that was looking at non-users of fabric conditioners and how to get them to try using the conditioners. When we ran our knowledge review, we realised we knew a lot about users, but not enough about non-users, which meant we had to do more research before deciding how to proceed with the project.

Knowledge review workshop plan (4-hour workshop)

Time	Task
09.00	▶ Welcome ▶ Introduce the objective ▶ Reminder of the creative behaviours
09.10	▶ As the workshop leader you will have collected all the contributions for the prep task, which was to review a report and interview a knowledgeable person using the fresh question templates ▶ Go around the room asking participants to introduce themselves ▶ Ask participants to walk around the room looking at the posters and collages ▶ Tell them to write notes on Post-its as they wander

185

Time	Task
09.30	▶ Split the team into five groups and give group 1 all the slides from fresh questions number 1, group 2 all the slides from question 2, etc. ▶ Ask them to think up themes for their prep task question, i.e. opportunities: 'we are ahead of our competition'; challenges: 'it is expensive to make' ▶ Teams present back their chosen theme ▶ The leader writes these down on separate pieces of paper
10.15	▶ Break
10.30	▶ Guest speaker presents their findings on how the company and competitors have been successful and where they could improve
11.15	▶ Split the team into five new groups ▶ Give each group one of the themes that was created in the prep task and review round ▶ Ask each group to produce five statements for ways to move forward using the information they have learned from the guest speaker as well as their prep task themes ▶ Ideally the group would consist of the person who originally presented the review themes combined with another two fresh people ▶ Each group presents their ideas back
12.00	▶ Rotate groups and give each group one of the ideas of ways to move forward ▶ Ask them to identify knowledge gaps within it ▶ Then work out an action plan, including timing and accountability
12.45	▶ Workshop leader talks through next steps and actions in light of the review ▶ Each team member writes a letter to themselves saying how they will move forward ▶ Closing comments
13.00	▶ Workshop ends

Ask yourself

▶ What sources do we have access to?

▶ How can we prevent people from being overwhelmed by the information?

▶ How can we incorporate visuals in our presentation?

▶ How will we break down the information into digestible chunks?

▶ How will we identify any knowledge gaps?

31

Debrief
workshops

> **Use for:** making the most of a debrief to create ideas and actions
>
> When your team have commissioned research from an outside agency, it is worth investing some time into making the debrief as productive as possible. Instead of people arriving at the last minute, checking their emails throughout and leaving at the end of the presentation, a few hours should be set aside for a debrief workshop session to embed the learning and create actions for the project to move forward.

The workshop objective: to make the most of a debrief by using active listening to structure and record implications

Bad call

A researcher once told me about presenting a big piece of quantitative research that had been commissioned by a large mobile phone company. He said that the client team spent the whole debrief checking their phones instead of listening to the work they had invested in.

Active listening tool

Consider what you want to answer at the end of the session and design an active listening task for the team to do during the presentation.

1 Ask the team to write Post-its as they listen. For example:

   ▶ What are the most important insights for our project?

> ▶ What should we improve before we continue with this project?

> ▶ What are the immediate next steps we should take?

2 Have flipcharts on the wall, one per question, during the presentation so the team remember what they are answering.

3 At the end of the debrief, ask team members to write their answers to the three questions (if they haven't already) before any discussion takes place. It's important to do this, otherwise the most dominant person in the room will begin the discussion and the others will not have a chance to record their thoughts.

4 Once everyone is ready, ask people to stick their Post-its on the relevant flipchart.

5 As the workshop leader you can collect these in themes per question, or place them randomly on the flipcharts and split the team up to summarise the Post-its for each question and present them back.

A debrief workshop structures feedback and next steps after a presentation and uses time wisely. It need not add too much time to the debrief – you can do the above task in just 10 minutes, or spend an hour working through the issues. It also makes sure the people in the room know what each other's views are, and are able to express those in the room rather than afterwards because they had to rush to another meeting.

Marketplace tool

For a more sophisticated debrief workshop, consider using the marketplace tool. It is very effective at creating energy and momentum, keeping people's attention and bringing insights to life.

1 Consider the different insights you want to bring to life, splitting them into three, four or five main sections (for example, three customer needs, four main insights, five winning ideas, etc.).

2 Assign each section a name and an area in the debrief room. Collect some images, quotes and slides that bring that section to life. Buy relevant stimuli (for example, if it's a type of consumer, buy the magazines that consumer would read and the products they would buy).

3 Write and rehearse a 10-minute script for each section and assign one presenter to each.

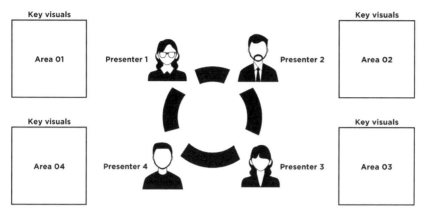

Marketplace

4 Lay out the room so that each section has a table and some wall space. Decorate each area with the name of the section, quotes, posters, images and slides on the wall and the materials on the table.

5 When the team members arrive in the room, split them into as many groups as there are sections, and ask each group to stand by one of the sections. Give them Post-it notes and pens.

6 Remind them they have 10 minutes at each station and that they should write ideas and implications for each before moving on.

7 Get the teams started, giving them a 10-minute presentation per section and rotating them after 10 minutes after they write down ideas and implications.

8 The presenters group and theme the ideas and implications and present them back to the whole workshop.

Why it works

▶ The power of this tool is in the movement, momentum and excitement it generates.

▶ By putting people in smaller teams, they pay more attention and ask more questions.

▶ The multi-sensory stimuli and pictures help them visualise the learnings.

▶ Having a task to do at the end (ideas, implications, etc.) means they listen with a focus on doing these tasks, making them more productive.

Debrief workshop plan (3-hour workshop)

Time	Task
09.00	▶ Welcome + objective + reminder of creative behaviours
09.15	▶ Split the team into four groups
	▶ Ask each group to stand by one of four sections set up around the marketplace room which each have a presenter
	▶ Ask people to carry with them Post-it notes and pens
	▶ Remind them they have 10 minutes at each station and that they will write down ideas and implications for each before moving on
	▶ Get the teams started, giving them a 10-minute presentation per section, rotating them after 10 minutes when they have written down ideas and implications
10.30	▶ Break
	▶ Presenters theme ideas and implications
10.45	▶ Workshop leader introduces the active listening questions and asks people to write down the answers as they listen to the presenters
	▶ Presenters from each group present their themes back
11.00	▶ Ask participants to make notes on each of the active listening questions individually and without discussion, and stick them on the relevant flipchart for that question
11.15	▶ Split team members into teams, with each team taking away one of the active listening questions to theme and summarise
	▶ Groups present back to each other
11.45	▶ Workshop leader talks through next steps and actions
	▶ Closing comments
12.00	▶ Workshop ends

Ask yourself

▶ How will you prevent people checking their phones during the session?

▶ How will you ensure people are actively listening and absorbing the information?

▶ What proportion of the time will you spend on debriefing and on next steps?

▶ How will you keep up the energy and momentum?

▶ How can you bring a presentation to life?

32

Virtual workshops

> **Use for:** running a workshop via video conference or conference call
>
> Ideally, workshops take place face to face. However, it is not always possible to have everyone in the same place. If you have to run a workshop via telephone or video conference, here are some guidelines to make the best use of the team's time.

The workshop objective: to prepare for and experience a high-quality workshop despite geographical distance

Preparation

1 Send a prep task for the team to read and carry out, like for any creative workshop, for example interviewing a stakeholder, conducting a mini case study, talking to a customer, etc.

2 Block relevant times in diaries to ensure time zones are matched and technical rehearsals are booked in.

3 If possible, do a technical rehearsal between all locations at the planned time of day and day of the week to assess signal strength, technical support and noise issues, and solve any problems well in advance of the session.

Principles

▶ Have one leader in each location who has rehearsed the plan with the workshop leader.

▶ Send the updates, presentations and stimuli in advance.

▶ Prepare very clear instruction slides for each section (translated into local languages if necessary).

▶ Have one note taker in each location typing up the outputs of each section of the plan live (translating into English if necessary).

▶ Spend 'live' time (in conference) for sharing, discussion and idea generation.

▶ Be live for an hour or less, with breaks in between to work in local breakout groups.

▶ Use time zones and overnight for teams to catch up with each other's ideas and share feedback.

▶ Set up guidelines for when technical issues occur (e.g. if we lose the video link, immediately dial in on a conference phone number, or call this mobile number).

Logistics

▶ Set up the live link one hour before the workshop.

▶ If on video conference, dial in on a conference phone number (which usually has a better sound quality) and mute the sound when you want images only.

▶ A shared presentation screen is helpful, so that all teams are following the right presentation and instructions.

Virtual workshop plan (9-hour workshop)

China	UK	Task
		Day 1
14.00	06.00	**Set up**
		▶ Test conference call and video conference link
		▶ Back up telecom line
		▶ Live test with slides
		▶ Check printing has been done in both locations
15.00	07.00	▶ Welcome and objectives
		▶ Way of working (immediately dial into conference call if signal drops, rules of engagement, not being on laptops, importance of being on time, etc.)
		▶ Principles and behaviours
		▶ Introductions and prep task
16.00	08.00	▶ Review of stakeholder interview and consumer comments and team's prep task (these have been sent in advance and summarised) and early ideas and comments
16.30	08.30	▶ Chinese consumer needs presentation
		▶ Break out (in smaller groups within each location) to create ideas and opportunities
		▶ Teams present back ideas
17.00	09.00	▶ Chinese market trends presentation
		▶ Overnight breakout: split local teams into new groups and instruct the teams to do one personal experience task overnight to inspire new ideas to present to each other on day 2
18.00	10.00	▶ Workshop ends
		Day 2
14.00	06.00	**Set up**
		▶ Test conference call and video conference link
		▶ Back up telecom line
		▶ Live test with slides
		▶ Check printing has been done in both locations
15.00	07.00	▶ Teams present ideas to each other and feed back on ideas
16.00	08.00	▶ Break
16.30	08.30	▶ Teams review all ideas before deciding on which to work on next
17.00	09.00	▶ Split into cross-location teams to work on the main ideas in small teams via conference call, developing them further together
		▶ Teams present back developed ideas
18.00	10.00	▶ Workshop leader talks through next steps and actions
		▶ Closing comments
19.00	11.00	▶ Workshop ends

Ask yourself

▶ Have you got the necessary technology in place for a virtual workshop?

▶ What tasks can you set to encourage teams in different places to share knowledge beforehand?

▶ Can you do a technical rehearsal before the session?

▶ How can you use time zones to your advantage?

33

Multilingual workshops

Use for: conducting workshops with people who speak different languages

Much of global business is conducted in English, and we assume that workshops will work well if everyone is speaking the same language, because that way we all understand each other in the moment. For a high quality of output, it is far better to allow people to speak in a natural and spontaneous way rather than speaking the same language.

Even in one language, ideas need time and stimulus to emerge. For participants with a language barrier, their contribution is limited and therefore the workshop outputs might be compromised, almost always working negatively against the non-English speakers. This gets in the way of alignment, because if people feel they have not been able to express themselves well enough, they will not feel their ideas are fairly represented.

The workshop objective: to lead a workshop that allows people to share ideas spontaneously, without being restricted by language differences

Multilingual workshops are about the preparation. Once the preparation is complete, run any one of the other session outlines. To prepare for a multilingual workshop:

▶ **Translation of prep tasks.** Stakeholders' and participants' prep tasks are done in the local language, then translated, themed and redistributed/presented in both English and the local language.

▶ **Materials in all languages.** Translate all introductions, objectives and materials into both languages, so that people can read along and you are not relying on a translator to get the nuances right.

▶ **Have translators present.** Have translators there to simultaneously translate between languages in all introductions, discussions for the day and ideas feedback.

▶ **Natural language groupings first.** Breakout groups can be organised by language (fluent English speaking vs non-English speaking) to allow working together to be spontaneous and comfortable, with feedback translated simultaneously.

▶ **Simultaneous ideas translation.** Develop multilingual templates for ideas, with languages represented next to each other on each template. When ideas are written in one language, they can then be translated into the others. By the end of the day, everyone will be able to read all the ideas in their own language.

▶ **Expert translation.** Rather than using commercial translators, try to use expert practitioners (leaders, researchers, concept writers, people familiar with the business) who are fluent in the local language to ensure the nuances are clear, rather than just translating the words themselves.

Ask yourself

▶ Will the ideas be better if people can speak in their own language?

▶ How many different languages will people be speaking at the workshop?

▶ How can you make use of prep tasks in people's own languages to inspire and prepare everyone before the workshop?

▶ How can you prepare guidelines and ways of working for the session to ensure everyone understands what is being asked of them?

▶ Are there cultural differences you need to consider within the team?

34

Workshop outputs

Use for: recording workshop outputs

Whether you are a workshop leader or participant it can be quite tempting to leave the workshop and go back to your job without recording ideas or taking away any actions. If you do this, people might not attend next time because they will not have seen any outputs.

The workshop objective: to deliver a record of the workshop outputs to the team members who took part

Whatever you decide to produce as an output, make sure the document is easy to understand, even by someone who was not at the workshop. This means beginning with the context, objectives and date, listing who participated and what the final ideas were.

Ways of producing workshop outputs:

▶ Take pictures of the flipcharts, templates and ideas, and put these into one presentation for people to flick through easily and to read this output again.

▶ Type up all the templates and ideas and send out the list of ideas to the team.

▶ Type up all the templates and ideas, then edit, improve and theme the best ideas, giving recommendations on ways forward.

▶ Bring the ideas to life with images, collages or graphic design so they are easy to understand.

▶ Produce a short film of the workshop, with interviews with key people, an overview of the day and a summary of the final ideas.

▶ Invite the team to a debrief workshop of the outputs.

In all outputs, try to remind people what the workshop was like by using photos of the event. This enhances their 'context dependent' memory, to remind people of the workshop and how they felt participating in it, not just the outputs themselves.

Underwater recall

A study on learning and memory with divers found that their word recall was significantly better when learned and recalled underwater, as opposed to learned underwater, recalled on land.[1] Evidence therefore suggests environmental cues, such as the context in which memories are formed, are very important.

Try to recreate the environment of the workshop in the same style of presentation with visuals, theming, and quotes and handwritten text from the people who attended. This will make the output contextually relevant and thus trigger the memory of what was learned on that day.

Dos and don'ts for outputs

Do:

▶ make output a priority, as this is a key responsibility of being a workshop leader

▶ put in half a day immediately after your session to write up and send out the ideas, or have a note taker assist you

▶ provide people with the output from the session (and thank them for their contribution) as soon as you can, otherwise you risk them not participating in future

▶ keep in mind that after about a week it becomes 'old news' – so if you plan to do something more ambitious, update people quickly with something simple and take more time to produce a more complicated output

▶ type up all of the ideas, not just the favourites – those ideas become a bank of resources later on

▶ structure the output so people see the final ideas first, then all the others

▶ take photos and put them in the output – it helps people to remember being in the session.

Don't:

▶ be a perfectionist with the output – it's better to send something that's rough than nothing at all

▶ throw away the templates, ideas or documents from the workshop for at least three months, as sometimes the original drawings or wording need to be checked.

Ask yourself

▶ Is the output easy to understand, even by someone who was not at the workshop?

▶ How can you bring the document to life?

▶ Why is the output important?

▶ How long after a workshop should you throw away the ideas/templates?

▶ How can you make producing the output easier while you are at the workshop?

A final word

I hope you are able to use this book to be a confident and well-prepared workshop leader, able to improve the productivity and creativity of the people around you. As you practise you will find ways of tailoring the methods in this book to suit your team, objectives and organisation. I look forward to hearing about some of the new tools you will create, the great workshops you will run and, most importantly, the new ideas you will make happen.

What did you think of this book?

We're really keen to hear from you about this book, so that we can make our publishing even better.

Please log on to the following website and leave us your feedback.

It will only take a few minutes and your thoughts are invaluable to us.

www.pearsoned.co.uk/bookfeedback

Tools list

Chapter 25

▶ Talk like me

▶ Four futures

Chapter 26

▶ Reasons why

▶ Dos and don`ts

▶ Old way, new way

Chapter 28

▶ Ideal job

Chapter 30

▶ Fresh questions

Chapter 31

▶ Active listening

▶ Marketplace

References

What this book will do for you

[1] Woolley, A. W., Chabris, C. F., Pentland, A., Hashmi, N. and Malone, T. W. (2010) Evidence for a collective intelligence factor in the performance of human groups. *Science*, 330(6004), 686–8.

Chapter 1: An introduction to workshops

[1] Miller, E. (2009) Interviewed by Jon Hamilton. Think you're multitasking? Think again. *NPR*. Retrieved from: http://www.npr.org/templates/story/story.php?storyId=95256794

[2] Schutt, R. (2010) *Consensus is not Unanimity: Making decisions cooperatively*. Cleveland, OH: The Vernal Education Project.

Chapter 2: The workshop approach

[1] Atherton, J. S. (2013) Convergent and divergent thinking styles. *Learning and Teaching*. Retrieved from: http://www.learningandteaching.info/learning/converge.htm

[2] Finke, R. A., Ward, T. B. and Smith, S. M. (1992) *Creative Cognition: Theory, research, and applications*. Cambridge, MA: MIT Press (Bradford Books).

Chapter 3: Setting the workshop objective

[1] Waldrop, M. M. (2011) Physics meets cancer: the disruptor. *Nature News*, 474(7349), 20–2.

Chapter 4: Who to invite to your workshop

[1] Woolley, A. W., Chabris, C. F., Pentland, A., Hashmi, N. and Malone, T. W. (2010) Evidence for a collective intelligence factor in the performance of human groups. *Science*, 330(6004), 686–8.

[2] Levine, S. S., Apfelbaum, E. P., Bernard, M., Bartelt, V. L., Zajac, E. J. and Stark, D. (2014) Ethnic diversity deflates price bubbles. *Proceedings of the National Academy of Sciences*, 111(52), 18524–9.

[3] Levine, S. S., Apfelbaum, E. P., Bernard, M., Bartelt, V. L., Zajac, E. J. and Stark, D. (2014) Ethnic diversity deflates price bubbles. *Proceedings of the National Academy of Sciences*, 111(52), 18524–9.

[4] Haltiwanger, J. (2015) Working abroad makes you more versatile, creative and successful. *Elite Daily*. Retrieved from: http://elitedaily.com/life/culture/working-abroad-versatile-creative-successful/1062445/

[5] Leonard, N. (2014) *Leadership and Collective Decision Making*. Paper presented at the Collective Intelligence Conference 2014, Massachusetts Institute of Technology, Boston, MA.

[6] Woolley, A. W., Chabris, C. F., Pentland, A., Hashmi, N. and Malone, T. W. (2010) Evidence for a collective intelligence factor in the performance of human groups. *Science*, 330(6004), 686–8.

Chapter 6: The workshop set-up

[1] Kouyoumdjian, H. (2012) Learning through visuals. *Psychology Today*. Retrieved from: www.psychologytoday.com/blog/get-psyched/201207/learning-through-visuals

[2] Coursey, D. A. (2012) *Language Arts in Asia: Literature and drama in English, Putonghua and Cantonese*. Newcastle upon Tyne: Cambridge Scholars Publishing.

[3] Lampe, N. (2014) Seeing is believing: the power of visual communications. *Hatch for Good*. Retrieved from: https://www.hatchforgood.org/explore/103/seeing-is-believing-the-power-of-visual-communications

[4] McMains, S. and Kastner, S. (2011) Interactions of top-down and bottom-up mechanisms in human visual cortex. *The Journal of Neuroscience*, 31(2), 587–97.

[5] Brenner, C. B. and Zacks, J. M. (2011) Why walking through a doorway makes you forget. *Scientific American*. Retrieved from: http://www.scientificamerican.com/article/why-walking-through-doorway-makes-you-forget/

Chapter 7: The workshop leader

[1] Hill, L. A., Brandeau, G., Truelove, E. and Lineback, K. (2014) Collective genius. *Harvard Business Review*, 92(6), 94–102.

Chapter 8: Workshop behaviours

[1] Woolley, A. W., Chabris, C. F., Pentland, A., Hashmi, N. and Malone, T. W. (2010) Evidence for a collective intelligence factor in the performance of human groups. *Science*, 330(6004), 686–8.

[2] Poldrack, R. (2010) Multitasking: the brain seeks novelty. *Huffpost Healthy Living*. Retrieved from: http://www.huffingtonpost.com/russell-poldrack/multitasking-the-brain-se_b_334674.html

[3] Miller, E. (2009) Interviewed by Jon Hamilton. Think you're multitasking? Think again. *NPR*. Retrieved from: http://www.npr.org/templates/story/story.php?storyId=95256794

[4] Atkin, N. (2012) 40% of staff time is wasted on reading internal emails. *The Guardian*. Retrieved from: www.theguardian.com/housing-network/2012/dec/17/ban-staff-email-halton-housing-trust

Chapter 11: Basic workshop tools

[1] Cherry, K. (2015) What is a heuristic? *About Health*. Retrieved from: http://psychology.about.com/od/hindex/g/heuristic.htm

Chapter 13: Creating quick ideas

[1] Woolley, A. W., Chabris, C. F., Pentland, A., Hashmi, N. and Malone, T. W. (2010) Evidence for a collective intelligence factor in the performance of human groups. *Science*, 330(6004), 686–8.

[2] What is creativity? (n.d.) *The Journey to Excellence*. Retrieved from: http://www.journeytoexcellence.org.uk/resourcesandcpd/research/summaries/rsfosteringcreativity.asp

[3] Csikszentmihalyi, M. and Csikszentmihalyi, M. (1991) *Flow: The psychology of optimal experience* (Vol. 41). New York: Harper Perennial.

[4] Butt, J. (1983) *James 'Paraffin' Young: Founder of the mineral oil industry*. Edinburgh: Scotland's Cultural Heritage.

Chapter 17: Creating a new story about something old

[1] Ciotti, C. (n.d.) The psychology of storytelling. *Sparring Mind*. Retrieved from: http://www.sparringmind.com/story-psychology/

Chapter 18: How to create new names

[1] Pratt, S. (2010) Ants compete, recruit to identify best colony (with video). *Phys Org.* Retrieved from: http://phys.org/news/2010-11-ants-colony-video .html

Chapter 19: Customer needs workshops

[1] Sparrow, B. (2014) *Creative and Analytical Thinking Online.* Paper presented at the Collective Intelligence Conference 2014, Massachusetts Institute of Technology, Boston, MA.

Chapter 22: Action planning

[1] Wax, D. (n.d.) The science of setting goals. *Lifehack.* Retrieved from: http:// www.lifehack.org/articles/featured/the-science-of-setting-goals.html

Chapter 23: Defining purpose

[1] Griffiths, R. (2015) Why is purpose important in the workplace? *The Association for Business Psychology.* Retrieved from: www.theabp.org.uk/news/ why-is-purpose-important-in-the-workplace.aspx

[2] Landreth, G. L. (2002) *Play Therapy: The art of the relationship.* New York: Brunner-Routledge.

Chapter 24: Working better together

[1] Sparrow, B. (2014) *Creative and Analytical Thinking Online.* Paper presented at the Collective Intelligence Conference 2014, Massachusetts Institute of Technology, Boston, MA.

Chapter 26: Positive turnaround

[1] Faberge, L. (2002) *Synectics Creative Teamwork.* London: Internal course manual.

Chapter 27: Team updates

[1] Couzin, I. D. and Krause, J. (2003) Self-organization and collective behavior in vertebrates. *Advances in the Study of Behavior,* 32, 1–75.

Chapter 29: Regular team meetings

[1] Faberge, L. (2002) *Synectics Creative Teamwork*. London: Internal course manual.

Chapter 34: Workshop outputs

[1] Godden, D. and Baddeley, A. (1975) Context dependent memory in two natural environments. *British Journal of Psychology*, 66(3), 325–31.

Index